Monsters Of Rock

The Unofficial History of the MOR Festivals at Donington Park

(Previously the first half of the book
'From Donington to Download: The History of Rock at Donington Park')

By
Ian Carroll

It has been an amazing journey producing this book, from cloudy Plymouth to rainy Holland to bright and sunny Donington Park; there has not been a dull moment in the last 9 years of writing this book, a book of blood, sweat & beers, many many beers……

After writing the Official Book of the Reading Festival it was time to make a start on the book of my other 'favourite' festival Donington Monsters of Rock - and as it is now – Download, the greatest rock festival the world has ever seen.

This book features over 300 interviews from major mega stars to small bands, to artists who are sadly no longer with us – included is an interview with the legend that was (and still is) Ronnie James Dio, who phoned me at home a week before he cancelled his last UK tour due to cancer, this is possibly one of his last interviews that he completed.

This book was a nightmare to produce, with publishers picking it up and dropping it due to the 'current book climate' and Live Nation being messed around by them as much as I was – though without the help of Andy, John & Stuart, I would not be where I am with this book today. I would also like to thank the journalist who sent me a couple interviews and the legendary Bailey Brothers who I did a few interviews with from when they were the DJ's, hosting the main stage and spinning discs between bands, great guys and still going!

Finally, thanks to all the 'festival attendees' who were interviewed for experiences over the years, they were great additions to the book.

So, the book is finally out as a Kindle published book, which is the way forward for new releases, though I don't rule out a printed copy in the future if another suitable publisher comes along.

Ladies and Gentleman, welcome to Donington Park

Dedicated to Raine, Nathan, Josh & Rex, the coolest little family that anyone could ever wish for

Introduction

If in deed it was true that Robert Johnson 'sold his soul to the Devil' in order to master the guitar and perform the most amazing blues music, then something similar must have occurred in Leicestershire in 1980 and every year since at the site of the Donington racetrack.

Selling their souls to the Devil in exchange for a weekend of Rock & Metal; thousands of similarly minded fans make the annual pilgrimage to Donington, for a weekend of every style of rock music available.

Donington has become the Mecca for 'metal heads' the world over, with people attending from as far afield as Australia for their annual fix of all that is best in the world of rock music.

From the initial Monsters Of Rock in the shadow of the Dunlop tyre to Download Festivals magnificent 'on form' show in 2009, nothing it appears can stop the metal beast from tearing up the countryside and laying waste to the ears of the thousands of punters in attendance.
With classic performances over the years from rocks giants such as AC/DC, Iron Maiden, Metallica and Kiss to the 'new school' of rock in the form of bands like Slipknot, Linkin Park, System of a Down and My Chemical Romance, the festival grows in stature and cult status each year.

The hallowed grounds of Donington Park are where most bands want to play and where most fans want to see them play. It's now developed into more than just a festival; it's an event, a gathering of similar minded people with a need to belong. A 'rock & metal brotherhood' where a feeling of 'family' and camaraderie is second to none. From the close knit community of the Official Download forums to the 'feel good factor' in the campsites, Download is now the place to be as a 'musical rite of passage' for thousands of people all over the world and with the increase in capacity, this extended family of rock is extending just that little bit more each year.

My first attendance at Donington was for Monsters Of Rock in 1983. I was there to see Whitesnake the most, with a dash of Twisted Sister and a sprinkling of Dio; with the rest of the line-up working well as an aperitif.

Living in Plymouth I had to travel over night each year, leaving Devon by coach at around midnight and eventually arriving at Donington at round 6am. It was usually cold, foggy and a place with nothing to do but drink, until the gates opened at around lunchtime. So after six hours or so of solid drinking, peeing in the woods and getting bored, it was down to the front of the 'bowl shaped' arena for a day of rocking out.

Every year that I attended Monsters Of Rock there were many 'stand out' moments; Motley Crue's first appearance in '84, Magnum's extremely British opening slot in '85, Metallica's debut also in '85, Cinderella playing in torrential rain in '87, Guns N' Roses over popular set in '88, Metallica's first headline slot in '95 and Kiss in full make up at the last Monsters Of Rock in '96; all classic sets and greatly appreciated by the fans, who heaved a great sigh when MOR died in '96, only to be re-born as Download Festival in 2003.

Download Festival has carried on the tradition that Monsters Of Rock had already established; amazing bands, fantastic times and best line-ups ever for a rock festival. Who could forget Metallica's secret set in '03 and their returning the following year without Lars and still pulling it off, Billy Idol returning to the UK to headline the 2nd stage in '05, Metallica playing

'Master Of Puppets' in its entirety in '06, Iron Maiden proving they were still the best British metal band in '07, Kiss proving they were still a massive festival band (with all the trimmings) in '08, the debut of the reformed Faith No More in '09 and the mighty return of Def Leppard 23 years since the last appearance to headline the final scorching day in '09. Again all amazing performances and thousands of other also; from the fourth to the mainstage the variety and choice of who to see and who not to see has never been better, but lets not mention the 'clashes'.

If you speak to any rock & metal bands in the world and ask 'which festival do you want to play at' their answer will always be the same, 'Donington'; ask the question to any rock fan 'which festival is the best one every year' and you get the same immediate reply 'Donington' (or Download depending on your age).

The festival has steadily developed into a weekend that now lasts nearly a full year. The Forums are teaming with people's memories of that year's festival from the day after it's all over up to about September. From September to January the forums are chock full of speculation about the following year's line-up and from January to June there is mass hysteria about the confirmed artists, about who's playing, who's not playing and those dreaded 'clashes', where a classic band that someone wants to watch on the mainstage clashes with a Norwegian Black Metal band that they want to watch on the 3rd stage, this frustration of course all gets directed at Andy Copping, because it's his fault. As we all must know, the booking of bands, on the scale that the festival has now reached, must be a real headache for Andy and of course there are going to be some clashes; but that's festivals for you and no one should be to blame.

With the increase in metal and rock festivals in Europe, such as Wacken Open Air, Hellfest, Sweden Rock, Graspop and of course now the European versions of Sonisphere, Download has still continued to flourish, building on it's success year after year and is still the dominant festival of its kind.

Over the next 25 chapters you will get a feel for the festival (if you have never been before), will be able to reminisce (if you have been to the festivals over the years) and you will get a full insight into the festival from not only the bands point of view, but also the fans and the organisers perspectives.

So, welcome to the Official Book of the Donington & Download Festivals and in the words of the Bailey Brothers:

'Rock Not Pop Metalheads!!!'

(Ian Carroll Author)

Forward by Mr Lars Ulrich, all the way from Brazil to my kitchen

"It's THE hallowed ground.
Over the 30 years, some of the best 'metal moments' have happened there; starting off with Rainbow and up through the AC/DC's and the Maiden's and the Whitesnake's and everybody else.
You could probably parallel the history of Donington to the history of rock.
Who's hot, who's was in, who was out, who moved up, who fell from grace; there's certainly a correlation between writing the history of Donington to writing the history of hard rock and metal.
To have been present six and a half times, it's certainly awesome to be part of the history of

something that I am extremely proud of and I really, really sincerely hope that Metallica will come back and play it again."
Lars Ulrich (Metallica – Drums)

1980
Rainbow
Judas Priest, Scorpions, April Wine, Saxon, Riot, Touch, Neal Kaye

August 16th 1980, a date that should be firmly noted in all diaries as a day of rock music celebrations; the day that the 'rock' was firmly embedded at Donington.

Prior to the inaugural festival in 1980, the only place that you could see rock & metal bands in the open, in the summer, was at Reading Festival. Though in the late '70's, Reading had strayed away slightly from rock music and had been covering New Romantic bands and up and coming new indie/punk bands such as the Police, Patti Smith and the Jam; the launch of a new music festival for 'out and out' rock fans was just was the doctor ordered.

Situated 'slap bang' in the middle of England, Donington Park racetrack seemed like the ideal location for a festival, equidistant to all travelling rock fans.

Organised by promoter Paul Loasby and Maurice Jones of MCP, they had the task of putting on what would become the longest running rock & metal festival in the UK.

The first year's line-up was a 'who's who' of rock giants, from Germany's finest Scorpions to Birmingham's 'Metal Gods' Judas Priest to the magnificent headliners Rainbow, who still featured two members of Deep Purple and were quite the draw on the day. This show was to be the last Rainbow performance for both Graham Bonnet and Cozy Powell; Bonnet left to pursue a solo career and then joining the Michael Schenker Group, Cozy Powell leaving to become drummer for Bonnet's solo project, then MSG and finally a full time member of Whitesnake, where he would return to Donington in 1983, again in a headline slot.

Added to this line up were Riot and Touch from New York and April Wine from Canada.

Touch had the honour bestowed on them of being the first ever band to play at the MOR Festival and the first band to play at Donington and certainly not the last!

Saxon were also on the bill, as part of the NWOBHM (New Wave Of British Heavy Metal). This was their first appearance and it had such an affect on them that they even wrote a song dedicated to their experience of the festival, 'And the Bands Played On'; this would not be their last performance at the festival.

One of the most bizarre moments of the festival was when a member of Touch, the opening act swallowed a bee onstage.

The Rainbow performance, or part of it, was broadcast by the BBC late at night, to the joy of rock fans everywhere

With an approximate attendance of 35,000 the festival, with a bargain ticket price of £7.50, was deemed a success, which paved the way for all future Monsters Of Rock festivals.

"I remember it being the best show that I had ever been on because, for one reason all my family were there and it was the first time they had ever seen the band play live. My Mum and Dad weren't really 'hard rock' fans, but they saw the show and they were just blown away.

It was a special treat for me and it was a very sad day at the same time because Cozy left and I was about to leave the same day too, but when he did leave it changed the whole atmosphere of the band, so later on I actually left myself. It was a great day and I will never forget it, ever.

I didn't think it was particularly one of the best shows we played musically, but there was something about it. The might have been a few rough edges here and there from everybody, but the crowd was fantastic

and it went very well. I remember it being a very long day.
I remember walking around in the afternoon a little bit, but we didn't really hang around the place very much at all.
We didn't get out of that place until about six the next morning, because there were so many people walking on the road, going wherever they were going. We got back to the hotel in Leicester and said goodbye to Cozy until he got into his car and drove away."
Graham Bonnet (Rainbow – Vocals)

"Playing at the Monsters of Rock Festival in Donington after Reading was vastly different for us - being that PRIEST in 1980 were no longer rookies - if anything we were the front runners of metal in the UK!!
That's why Donington being all out rock and metal was the ultimate gig at the time for us!! It was the one we just had to play.
I can remember feeling immensely proud to be up there banging my head with thousands of metal heads in sync with us!! Donington attracted the cream of metal bands from all over the world. And I am sure I can speak for all of the bands and all of the fans when I say that there should be a Donington every single weekend!!"
K.K. Downing (Judas Priest – Guitar)

"I do remember it was a special moment for us in time. I remember it was great to play with the Scorpions and Saxon and Rainbow as well. It was

just a great festival line-up and I have very fond memories of it."

What does stick in my mind was that we had some serious pyrotechnics to let off and for some reason we weren't allowed to, I don't know why it was. They were serious fireworks and they were in 3 foot tubes and we had to set them off were car batteries. As we didn't set them off, we shared them out between us.

We saved them until bonfire night and dished them out and we all had an incredible firework display. I remember I lived in a little village in Staffordshire; I let mine off and the police arrived within 10 minutes because they thought someone had let bombs off and it was pretty spectacular and the loudest noise I'd ever heard."

Glenn Tipton (Judas Priest – Guitar)

"Thinking about Donington, it was not only an amazing bill, in 1980 there were bands like Judas Priest, Rainbow, etc., it was also a very memorable moment, with five Germans racing (on their way to the stage) round the legendary Donington Speedway in the wrong direction. Can you imagine the expression on the face of our driver / Tour manager Bob Adcock (Liverpool) facing a bunch of motorbikes coming at high speed towards us around the corner. Well, the Scorpions survived."

Scorpions

"I forget exactly the year we were there but it was in the early '80's. 1982 I think. The day we were there was sunny and dry. The first dry day of Donington that year. The grounds were soaked. Soft, sticky mud

everywhere backstage and out front.
The backstage crew had put straw down on the ground to try and soak up the moisture but with the grass turning to mud, the straw just added to the problem and footwear was caked with straw and mud to the point of making everyone's feet look huge!
We were all issued rubber boots or Wellingtons as I think the British call them.
I brought mine home to Canada and used them for many years. Must be the Scot in me.
The dressing rooms were quite some distance from the stage and we were driven there by kamikaze young drivers.
The road to the stage was dirt and rather bumpy and those mad shuttle pilots choose to go as fast as possible.
We almost threw our driver out and drove ourselves. It was that bad!
Rainbow was the headliner that day. I wasn't a fan as much as I am today. It was Cosy Powell's last show with them.
I wish I had stayed to watch him and Ritchie Blackmore. I know I missed something special.
Everyone backstage and out front was in dressed in black except us. At that time we were wearing red and white and all our Marshall amps were red with white grill cloth. Did we stick out in an embarrassing way? Yes! We played our songs to a very wet crowd of mud men. Not all, but enough to remember it that way.
Our big hit at the time in the USA and Canada was a love ballad called "Just Between You and Me". To me

that worked in North America but not that day. It was a Heavy Metal crowd and we looked like a damn pop band. I remember feeling a tad out of place playing that tune.

We had some heavy songs that rocked like "Crash and Burn" "Before the Dawn", "Sign of the Gypsy Queen', but in England we were billed as a Heavy Metal band compared to the USA and Canada where we were known as a Hard Rock Band. England took their metal seriously!

It might have been me feeling out of our element that day or it might have been it was just Rainbow's day, but I never really came away with good memories of our performance at Donington.

If it came to do it again, I would in a flash, but without the red and white which was gone the next year anyway.

I'm glad I was part of Donington's long history."

Brian Greenway (April Wine – Guitar/Vocals)

"The first time was fantastic. Obviously it was the first major metal festival in England, maybe Europe actually, but definitely in Britain.

We were one of the rising stars then of the '80's metal scene and they asked us to play it. We'd had a very big album released previously, 'Wheels Of Steel', so it was great walking onstage in front of 60,000 people that all knew the songs; that was a new thing for us, we'd never experienced that before.

I think it really broke us bigger, because we weren't the same as other bands on there. We were looked on as a 'newer rising act' and bands like Rainbow, Judas Priest and Scorpions were established acts.

It was really great; it was a special festival where the audience wanted to see everybody."

I went for a ride on Rob Halfords Harley-Davidson around the track, he didn't know though!

We watched all the bands because then it was different; the festival was in the field and the dressing rooms were in the pit lane. There wasn't much down at the stage actually.

Our agent booked all the bands and we were earmarked to become big. We came on in the afternoon, which isn't always a good thing, but the reviews were actually really good for us 'we should have been on later', 'they stole the show' and all that sort of silliness, but we really enjoyed it"

Biff Byford (Saxon -Vocals)

"In 1980 it was announced to us that we had been booked for Donington a new festival; this was a good year for us as 'Wheels Of Steel' and two singles both did great and we were selling out everywhere,

When we arrived, the dressing rooms were miles from backstage so we settled into our room. We had a balcony overlooking the courtyard below and Judas Priest was doing a photo shoot in full metal regalia with Rob looking like a 'Metal God'. A few weeks before we had done a 7-week tour with them and Top Of The Pops so we went down to say hi and noticed a few people from other bands snickering at Rob in his gear; but they had the smile wiped off their faces when Priest hit the stage.

Fortunately the set from Saxon was preserved on audio and listening to a new version recently (09) mastered at Abbey Road by EMI, it's easy to see why this is the penultimate Saxon line up of the 5 original members with Pete Gill hammering the drums relentlessly and I in true Metal tradition destroyed my Stratocaster in 'Machine Gun'.

All the bands and liggers used a shuttle bus to the back stage area and I sat opposite to Joe Elliot who was sporting black and white trousers striped he was going down to catch our set as at that point he had not seen us or us them and were both curious to see the competition (but he was just a guest).

The roar of the crowd when we hit the stage was unforgettable and when Gilly and Dobby were playing the sing back part in 'Bap Shoo Ap' the beat from just two was like a steam hammer and I remember thinking 'this is Metal Woodstock.

After our set I was going to watch the Scorpions when a Mercedes pulled up right behind the stage and the window came down. I heard Graham and it was Ritchie Blackmore shouting me over and he spoke as though we were old friends he said we did a great set and he also said I cannot tell you have a handicap (like Tony Iommi I have a finger end missing). He told me he had seen Hendrix at the Isle Of White Festival ten years before and he signed my program 'To Graham' which I still have to day. We chatted a while and he wished me well and off he went to his private room, but I had never spoke to him before.

At this time we did not know that Donington, the first one, would become the iconic festival it has become or that the following years it would become the most famous metal gig of all. It was only when we met people like Lars, Dimebag and Motley Crue; they all asked about 'wow what was the first Donington like?' and it was great to tell the story to so many musicians and fans."

Graham Oliver (Saxon – Guitar)

"Well, while things were brewing in the States with our singles "When The Spirit Moves You" and "Don't You Know What Love Is" our manager Bruce Payne got us on a tour with Rainbow and we were off to Europe to open up. Quite memorable being on tour with the guitar player of my favorite band "Deep Purple" to say the very least.

One show, Monsters of Rock Live At Donington, turned out to be more than we could have ever imagined. We arrived on a rainy, muddy day at the huge racetrack to open up the show, which featured Rainbow, Judas Priest, Scorpions, Riot and April Wine. Without knowing it at the time, we became the first band ever to play at Monsters of Rock Festival.

There was a sea of faces (60,000 people I was told)...almost as far as we could see...and I remembered what someone said...if you can get the front 5,000 people, you are good to go. I think it went really well, though no sound check...anyway, the audience responded great, though they had never heard of us before, mainly we focused on performing the songs properly. Tapes I've heard since, we sound spot on...the harmonies, etc. though it's hard to resist playing the songs a tad faster when the adrenalin is rushing thru you... What was interesting was, the mayhem that followed with all the other bands, we were fortunate to have been set up and ready to go (e.g. bass drum mic on *the bass drum and guitar mic on the guitar, rather than on something else) because changing mics and channels, etc. through the day was a great challenge for the crew. This definitely helped when it came to mixing the "live" LP that was released. When I got off stage there was quite a commotion, rumours that our bass guitar player had maybe possibly swallowed a bee. That event seems to have overshadowed the entire day, the music, the two years of striving to get to that stage, kind of surreal really...and it was a good lesson to us.*

Anyway "Don't You Know What Love Is" became #1 on the Melody Maker

chart and there was Doug on the front page of Melody Maker holding the plastic cup from which he says he may have swallowed the bee. Is this Spinal Tap, or what?

We ended up using the live performance on a live CD of the show and, to his credit, Roger Glover, who produced the LP, wouldn't let us overdub or change the originally recorded tape...an honest moment... though we would have loved to have added our 30 part harmonies and walls of keyboards (I only have two hands and this was before sequencing, samples and all that). When I heard the CD I saw other bands hadn't quite been as "reserved" in their approach, but it was cool and sounded OK. Anyway, proud to have done it, proud to have been there, look back at it with a huge smile on my face...would love to do it again...loved the time, the vibe, the musicianship, the values...all good stuff..."

Mark Mangold (Touch – Keyboards / Vocals)

"The funny thing about Donington was that when I was with Motorhead and Doug Smith Management, he was trying to put something on at Donington but Maurice Jones from MCP nipped in behind him and got the rights to Donington, so we were there right at the beginning, but that was why we did Port Vale. We were going to play Donington!"
Fast Eddie Clarke (Motorhead - Guitar)

"I was present at Cozy Powell's final gig with Rainbow, spending time with him in the afternoon, meeting Ritchie Blackmore for the first time, I was sorry to see CP leaving the band, I always thought that Rainbow were one of the metal bands, and CP was a vital ingredient of the band."
Bernie Marsden (Whitesnake – Guitar)

"The first one that I went to was the first one that was headlined by Rainbow in 1980.
I was actually just out in the audience; I went with Sean Harris and Colin Kimberley the bass player.
It was a good gig and we particularly enjoyed Rainbow as that was who we had mainly gone to see and Judas Priest were on. Priest were good on the day and I remember them doing 'You Don't Have To Be Old To Be Wise'."
Brian Tatler (Diamond Head – Guitar)

"I remember very vividly as a kid, looking at the Donington posters and thinking one day I will play that (the year that Rainbow headlined in particular) I think Judas priest played that year also."
Myke Gray (Skin – Guitar)

"We feel privileged to be a part of the history of the Donington Monsters Of Rock festival.
We were there at the very first Monsters Of Rock in 1980. We thought we had a great vantage point looking down over the crowd underneath a Union Jack with Sheffield proudly painted across it. The view was great but the sound was awful. Half the music just disappeared up a cow's arse a mile down the road due to a swirling wind. It was like watching a video out of sync (The gig not the cow's arse).
Saxon were good, so were the Scorpions, but Rainbow was fuckin' awesome. Graham Bonnet looked like he had just come from a wedding party but what a voice.
You have to applaud Paul Loadsby (promoter) who was brave enough to stick his arse on the line to give us Rock and Metal fans a festival we could finally call our own. Helped out by another legend in the rock promoter circus Maurice Jones of MCP (Midland Concert Promotions)."
The Bailey Brothers (Mick & Dez Donington Comperes)

"The first ever 'Monsters of Rock' at Castle Donington, was to be my first ever experience of a gig, and to be honest, as a naïve 16 yr old, I don't remember that much of the actual performances, it was the experience as a whole.
The red double decker bus ride from Broadmarsh Bus station to the venue, buzzing with anticipation. The sight of the gathering crowd outside the gates. Once inside, I was blown away by the sea of people,

the stalls, the plethora of colours, the smells (some very suspect!!!!) and the mud bath!

I vividly recall a group of fans skidding and sliding up and down the field, left of stage, to uproars, and ovations, plastered from head to toe in sludge.

It was a day where I heard the sentence "OK you bad ass M. F's..." more times than I care to mention....And the portaloo experience, which I'd rather forget.....the queues, my fear of getting lost........oh, and Rainbow, a classic performance of 'Since you've Been Gone'.

Fond, fond memories."

Jane Bartley (Plymouth)

"I attended all 15 of the 'Monsters of Rock' festivals at Castle Donington.

I am probably fortunate that I was at the right age at the time of the first festival (17 years old) to be able to go on to attend all the festivals. In fact (although a little sad in hindsight) during the 80s it was my highlight of the year each year.

I would organise the tickets, the transport (5 of us in a Ford Cortina in 1980 to 20 of us in two transit vans in '87 and '88), the banners & flagpoles (these became more ambitious every year with flags and flashing lights etc being added each year, some people actually used our flagpoles as meeting points), and of course........the beer. Over the years the rules for which containers you could use for carrying your beer in changed from using virtually whatever you liked to not being able to use anything at all, but the daftest idea was probably when you could use a 2-litre bottle as long as the top and neck had been cut off, this made it almost impossible to carry when full.

Most people would probably say that spending all day in a mostly muddy (Donington was famed for its mud way before Glastonbury) field with up to 100 thousand denim and leather clad rockers listening to a sometimes inaudible racket was their version of Hell, but to me it has given me some of the greatest memories of my life and I am proud to claim that I attended them all and loved every minute of it.

In 1980 I had never attended an outdoor festival before, so my excitement was at fever pitch during the preceding week, especially as my all-time hero (still is to this day) Ritchie Blackmore would be headlining. There were all sorts of rumours about Blackmore playing a major solo on top of the speaker stacks way above the stage (as it happened this didn't take place due to some mechanical lift failure apparently).

My very first view of Donington (and my earliest memory) was as we approached the entrances from the car park I could see the merchandise stalls from afar with the Rainbow 'Down to Earth' knitted scarves pinned to the top of the marquees. I had missed out on one of these scarves from the tour earlier in the year, so my wallet was honed into buying one as soon as we got in. I still have it today (along with all the festival t-shirts and programmes from every year).

I also recall that there was a Greenpeace stall, selling 'what else' but 'Rainbow Warrior' t-shirts. There was also an official Rainbow fan club stall on site.

Musically the highlight of the day (and probably of any day) was the way Rainbow segued 'Since You

Been Gone' into 'Somewhere Over The Rainbow' and then straight into 'Stargazer' (my favourite song ever)....even though Graham Bonnet did mess the words up a bit. Cozy Powell's '1812 overture' drum solo went off with its usual bang and Blackmore's (stage managed) setting fire to a speaker stack during his guitar onslaught finale were other fond memories of the headlining act.

I remember getting into a queue for a burger approx 20 minutes prior to Judas Priests' set and still being stood in the same place in the queue some one and a half hours later after they had left the stage. I think the stallholder must have been a Priest fan.

To me Scorpions were playing as well as they ever did at that time in their career (prior to the MTV-friendly version we got a few years later) and their set was as faultless as ever (I saw them 3 times during 1980). I recall 'Pictured Life' being a particular favourite of mine at the time.

Saxon were also on a roll on the back of their nationwide 'Wheels of Steel' tour. They went down very well.

Of the other bands I can only really remember April Wine being ok.

The weather on the day was fine, but the preceding fortnight continuous rain had made the site a mudbath.

The toilets were appalling!!!"

Paul Hartshorn (Chesterfield)

"I have to admit I don't remember a whole lot about the bands as this was my first festival and I was just

caught up in the atmosphere of the whole thing. However, this is what I can remember.

Saxon, who were the first band I ever saw live, were at their peak and put in a decent set, including their 2 biggest hits 'Wheels of Steel' and '(747) Strangers in the Night' fronted by my neighbour from Barnsley Pete 'Biff' Byford. I remember Biff lived in a 2-up 2-down terrace house at the time but rode the biggest motorbike I'd ever seen which must have been worth as much as the house.

Speaking of motorbikes, there was a huge roar from the crowd when Rob Halford took to the stage on a Harley although if memory serves there was some confusion at first as Halford had changed his hair colour/style for the gig and for a few seconds some people were in a panic that Halford had been replaced by someone else. Scorpions were as brilliant as they've always been in the dozen or so times I've seen them. Klaus Mein's 'Hello Donning Castle' was classic Klaus.

Rainbow were awesome instrumentally but Rick Astley look-a-like Graham Bonnet's voice could never match Dio's live. Blackmore was his usual tease, giving little snippets of classic Purple/Rainbow songs, so when he started playing 'Stargazer' we all thought we'd just get a few bars as he'd always said it was too complicated a song to reproduce live. When we realised they were ACTUALLY GOING TO PLAY 'STARGAZER' the whole placed erupted! It still brings chills to my spine 30 years later.

I was on such a high from the whole day that I didn't care that I was caked in mud, we missed our last bus home, had to sleep under a tree by a river which I fell

into in the middle of the night and then spend the early hours of Sunday morning wandering around Derby to find a launderette to dry my clothes. It was one of those days that I'm privileged to say that 'I was there'."
Tony Nixon (Plymouth)

"The best experience I ever had at Donington park was at the first ever Monsters of rock Saturday 16th August 1980. Back then I was 18 and it was my first ever festival.

I attended it with my good friend Robert Tosh, who sadly isn't with us anymore. RIP. He was 24 and decided to take me with him to Donington. I remember every detail of the experience we started by getting the overnight Liverpool boat on the Thursday in order to be there for Friday, we then got the train to Crewe, and then travelled from Crewe to Derby. We dropped our stuff off at the Redsetters guest house and went off to buy our Monsters of Rock tickets. (Which I still have, it's proudly framed and hung on the wall as its one of my most prized possessions). I can still remember that the ticket only cost us £7.50 each, which is unreal considering the bands we got to see live.

On the Saturday we got the bus into Donington Park, it was a sunny day, but the fields were covered in muck, but that didn't matter we just couldn't wait to see all the bands on stage. I always thought it was amazing how between each bands performance instead of having music playing in the background they had DJ Neal Kay playing.

Throughout the performances of the bands that played there, there are a couple of moments that will always stand out to me.

Saxon on stage playing '747' and 'Wheels Of Steel', the crowd went nuts.

Rob Halford walking out on stage dressed head to toe in leather and studs milking the crowd, and then cracking his whip straight into the intro song and KK Downing, ripping away on his flying V guitar to 'Sinner'.

One of the main highlights was definitely when the main headliner RAINBOW were to appear on stage, their intro music soared through the sound system, and as soon as they appeared on stage I was lifted about 30-40ft forward because of the surge of the crowd and ended up at the very front of the stage, I couldn't believe I was so close to these rock n roll legends.

From then I attended Donington until 1984, then travelled back again in 2008 and 2009 for Download. I'm now 48 and still a loud and proud metal head."

John Dickson (Belfast)

1981
AC/DC

Whitesnake, Blue Oyster Cult, Slade, Blackfoot, More, Tommy Vance DJ

Back for another year and another amazing line-up.
With AC/DC making their first headline appearance at Donington the festival was bound to be a success. Coming off the commercial

triumph that was 'Back In Black', several songs from the album littered the set, including 'You Shook Me All Night Long', 'Hells Bells' and the albums title track. Now with Brian Johnson, accepted by all the fans, at the helm on vocals, after Bon Scott's death in 1980, AC/DC were slowly becoming one of the most popular and biggest rock bands in the world. They remain the band that is most linked with the Donington festivals from the beginnings of MOR to Download; 2010 will be their 4th slot at the festival, a joint record for Donington headline appearances equalled by Iron Maiden.

Whitesnake were in the special guest spot and they were becoming bigger with each release. They had recently brought out the 'Come an' Get It' album, hitting the UK album charts and spawning the singles 'Don't Break My Heart Again' and 'Would I Lie To You'.

Elsewhere on the bill Blue Oyster Cult weren't having a good day and as Joe Bouchard put it *'it was probably the worst show in BOC history'*; drummer fired in the morning, poor sound and Eric Bloom going crazy on his plaque (read on for his account of the day).

Slade played before BOC with toilet rolls in large quantities being thrown into the crowd from the stage and vice versa. Noddy and the boys were at the time having a 'second wind' due to their successful slot at Reading Festival the previous year, where they were last minute replacements for Ozzy Osbourne. Unfortunately Slade played during the worst rain of what ended up being a somewhat wet day.

Blackfoot played their brand of Southern Rock, with Rickey Medlocke on lead vocals and guitar; Medlocke now plays guitar for the ultimate Southern Rock band Lynyrd Skynryd.

The opening slot this time was given to More, another band that had been added to the ever increasing category of NWOBHM bands, flooding venues up and down the UK at the time. Laurie Mansworth, lead guitarist of More, went on to manage Roadstar who opened the 2006 Monsters Of Rock festival at the Milton Keynes Bowl; Roadstar have now transformed into Heaven's Basement.

Another year was over, a very wet year and the first to feature the Radio One DJ Tommy Vance as the shows compere; Tommy hosted the Friday night Rock Show on Radio One from 1978 to 1993. 'TV On The Radio' was the new voice of Monsters of Rock at Donington for the next 5 years.

"The first one I worked was with AC/DC in 1981, which was as cracker."
David Coverdale (Whitesnake – Vocals)

"I have very fond memories of Donington. I played in 1981, as I am sure you are aware on the AC/DC bill. I regard the show as the most memorable of festival gigs, even though we were not headliners. On the day we felt very pleased to say the least, the crowd were amazing and I felt that our recent return

from the USA had been very personal from the vast UK audience. Backstage I remember one thing very clearly. Those US people from Blue Oyster Cult deemed that they were "disrespected" on the bill, and took great pleasure smashing their memento mounted posters from Maurice Jones the promoter, Maurice had made one for each member of every band, a nice gesture, I still have mine. The BOC guys said they were making their point, but the only people that saw their act were other members of bands on the bill, of whom all just looked at one another and shrugged, "Americans".... On stage I personally remember looking out from the stage and realizing the crowd was as big in width as it was in length, and that shook me a little, word has it that 140,000 could have been there that day, well I believe it. I continued a friendship with Rick Medlocke, now in Lynryd Skynyrd, he was in Blackfoot when I first encountered him at a radio station in Nottingham the night before."
Bernie Marsden (Whitesnake – Guitar)

"1981 was BOC's only Donington appearance, part of a larger tour of the UK, having played in Dunstable, W. Runton and London a few days before.
The headliner was AC/DC, an act that had opened for BOC in the USA previously but was now undeniably a bigger band. My memories of this day haven't faded much since it was the same day our drummer was let go, but that's another story.
The drum roadie, Rick Downey, drummed his first 'real' show with us...quite a first gig, in front of 70,000 people. If you're running the often-used photo of me

jumping on the festival plaque, that would tell a lot, but not the whole story. Of course, I don't have the same perspective as the AC/DC folks (and by the way, I love AC/DC's music, great band) but as I recall there was some bad blood on their part about some slight when they opened for us somewhere in the USA, not getting all our lighting system or something like that. (It's quite standard practice that the headliner doesn't allow the opening act to have the entire lighting system at their disposal, i.e. when we opened for Alice Cooper (a legend who should be in the R&R Hall of Fame) we got some lights, not all, but that's quite normal and we didn't cop an attitude about it).

I showed up at Donington and was told straight off that AC/DC's folks weren't allowing us to use a motorcycle on stage (a gag that I often did in those days). Ok...so right away things were stirring. We finally get into our set and after a few songs our soundman uses his talkback from the mixing desk telling us to play 'Reaper' immediately and get off...the sound system wasn't working for us and no one could hear a thing we were doing. I immediately thought 'sandbag'...an oft-used term for the headliner's sound people ruining the sound of opening acts, like only using half the system or worse. Hard to believe, but this was stuff that would happen on occasion, not unknown.

It was a tough day...first our drummer was fired in the morning, the attitude I received upon arriving at the grounds, then sounding terrible in front of a festival with 10's of thousands of fans.

To take out my frustration I took the plaque given to all the band members and laid it across a rock and stomped on it. Impetuous youth, perhaps :) Our sound man George Geranios can tell the sound story on his own and his perspective is an important part of the whole festival. Nowadays, I love playing the UK, always did except for that one unfortunate afternoon 26 years ago."
Eric Bloom (Blue Oyster Cult – Vocals/Guitar/Keyboards)

"It was not the best show for us. There has been much discussion of that concert with fans on the web.
It seems it all started as a tiff we had with AC/DC's management when they denied letting us use of pyro and our motorcycle onstage. With that rumbling behind the scenes and the replacement of our drummer the day before the show, and the sabotaged sound system, it was probably the worst show in BOC history."
Joe Bouchard (Blue Oyster Cult – Bass)

"In 1981 the Castle Donington music fest featured the bands More, Blackfoot, Slade, Blue Oyster Cult, Whitesnake and AC/DC. The weeks leading up to this appearance had been stressful for the Oysters. Serious internal problems had developed between Albert Bouchard and other band members. They ostensibly revolved around Albert's choice of travelling mate, a young lady who was not his current wife. Band wives in the party were incensed. Tensions were high. Albert and his paramour

travelled separately and he was late for two shows. He was summarily fired just before the band was to play the main event on this English run: the massive Donington show. Up to 60,000 are expected to attend. Rick Downey (the lighting designer) had stepped in earlier in the week when Albert was late. He was now tapped to do the show rather than have the band suffer a humiliating cancellation. Given the subsequent events, perhaps a cancellation would have been better. At the time, however, we thought we had found a clever solution for the sudden departure of the band's drummer on the eve of this hugely important English festival. Bands would come to Donington Park a day before the actual concert. The first day was for sound and equipment checks. Various wrinkles were ironed, stage space was allocated, and input lists were checked and implemented. Ideally all the bands were given a chance to play a song or two through the sound system. Settings for monitors and front-of-house could be logged for recall the next day so that the band techs were not starting "cold." The sound contractor for this festival was Malcolm Hill. Hill Audio was a well-known native company based in Hollingbourne, UK in the great Tradition of the Times the company was named after, owned and run by Malcolm Hill. Malcolm and his employees designed and purpose-built a great deal of the equipment in his own shop. Speaker cabinets, power amplifiers and mixing consoles were all custom made and proprietary.

We arrived the day before for our sound check and set up the gear. I ambled out to the mix position and begin to set input levels. I remember trying to reset Joe Bouchard's bass direct level at the console. For some reason I did not have enough range on the channel's input attenuator. I was surprised when I was informed that the console had only a limited range of adjustment and a call had to be made back to the stage to set another level control there. This, I felt, was a less than ideal system but a lot of Hill's gear was like this. The speakers themselves were a custom one-box design with several new elements. This show was to be the debut of this new design. A wall of these untried boxes flanked each side of the stage.

I remember that despite my unfamiliarity with the console the sound check went OK. The system, though not thrilling, was adequate. There certainly was enough of it up there to make a big noise. However, those who play Donington as support soon learn not to count their decibels before they hatch. The day arrives. We in the Cult Camp were in a state. It was Rick Downey's first huge show. The audience was quite large, something like 60K. It was, of course, a miserable day of overcast skies and intermittent rain. There was schism regarding our use of the motorcycle gag. AC/DC said we couldn't do the motorcycle thing because they are doing the motorcycle thing. The situation (I learned later) got heated. There were bad vibes in the air. I, however, must perform my hour or so of work so I trudged dutifully to the front of house position. I don't really remember exactly when I went out. It may have been during Blackfoot's set. I know I was there for the entirety of Slade's set. At some point it was evident

that something was wrong with the system. Things did not sound good. Things did not sound right. It was not simply 'operator error.' In the old days the only real qualification for getting work as a live sound mixer was having the job. Power was (and still is) put in the hands of fools. "Hey, my brother-in-law once owned a stereo. He can be our sound guy!" This was not that. This mix was OK, the system itself sounded wrong.
I remember distinctly, I was standing in back of the mix riser and a fellow emerged from the vast mass of soggy humanity. He was quite upset. He got my attention and said, "Is Blue Oyster Cult going to sound this bad?" I said, "I hope not." Optimism, however, was fleeing. Toward the end of Slade's set the sound simply disappeared. Noddy, the lead singer, realized something had gone wrong. I remember that he launched into something obviously quite familiar to the assembled horde and, surprisingly, got most of the audience singing along! Perhaps it was their BIG HIT. I think it was their last song. It was now the Cult's turn. There was much consternation during the set change. No one seemed to know exactly what the problem with the system was, but we all knew there was a problem. We started the set and there was very little volume available. The sound check settings produced an anaemic squeak from the huge mass of boxes flanking the stage. At some point during the set I looked up to see Malcolm Hill himself crawling around the stage right stack at a great height, ears into boxes. I was told not to try to turn the system up,

but the band is inaudible. I try anyway and as I push the main faders up, the system volume decreases even more! Things are upside down, and I would be upside down if I tried that again, so said my minders at the front of house. At one point during this farce I got on the talkback mike between songs and told the band to simply leave the stage. Maybe they could come back out when things were sorted. If they continued without acknowledging the problem then our Donington appearance would be shot. They do not do this and our Donington appearance is shot. The Band finishes with a flourish and…….there is nothing. No response from the audience. Sixty-thousand metal fans stand sullen and silent. It is, as they say, an oil painting out there. As interesting as the actual performance was, some of the later developments were fascinating. Jake Berry, AC/DC's production manager took on the role of damage control for the band and Malcolm Hill and apparently told the assembled press that I blew up the system. As you can see from this account,
the system was already in deep trouble well before B.O.C.'s set. Let us consider the essence of the definition of "blow up." It is to destroy and hence render <u>inoperable</u>. By most accounts the system was fully operational by AC/DC's set. It was rendered inoperable by a basic power distribution problem, a mobile recording truck had apparently been hooked up improperly and the main system had "dropped a leg." In laypersons terms, the system was running on inadequate and unbalanced power. This fact did not alter Berry's spin, as senseless at it was on closer inspection. Year's later, when he was with

Whitesnake and I was with Anthrax, he bent my then girlfriend's ear at a show in the US, describing me as a bad guy, a representative of Satan, and who knows what else. Tell the same lie often enough and it becomes the truth.
The Band survived this debacle to move on to other debacles in other large venues: dare I say Pasadena Rose Bowl with Journey or shows in Germany with Whitesnake (where our own sound company "sandbagged" us). These "festivals" always bring out the knife sharpeners. I believe the band bled for a long time in the UK due to this. But in the end it isn't useful to discuss who was at "fault." It was a big, complicated show and something went wrong. There was an error and, unfortunately the audience didn't get all the show they paid for."
George Geranios (Blue Oyster Cult – Sound Engineer)

"I went as a guest to all the other Doningtons and was at the side of the stage for AC/DC the following year and the fire works at the end were awesome.
By this time we had wrote 'And The Bands Played On' all about Donington '80. I came up with a riff Quinny the chorus and Dobby, Biff AND Gilly did the words; a team effort which proved to be a top twenty hit rising to 12 and we performed our tribute to Donington on Top Of The Pops."
Graham Oliver (Saxon – Guitar)

"I first went to Castle Donington in 1981, aged 15, and 5 foot nothing, with my older brother.

We somehow got separated while in line at the fried chicken stand between Blackfoot and Slade. The rest of the day I spent alone in a crowd of 30,000 metalheads. My innocence hid the fact they were mostly drunk or stoned. Never once did I feel I didn't belong or was in any danger. I was ok; I still had enough sandwiches and pop to last me.
Not that I could see, but soon there would be, live onstage, 2 of the bands which had turned my life around and given it meaning, Whitesnake and AC/DC. All the songs I knew word for word and would scream the lyrics without seemingly being heard over the deafening PA.
Fireworks over, I turned and headed for the Goodyear Tyre.
Near the top of the hill I saw the familiar patched combat jacket of my older brother. I ran up to him.
"What did you think?"
"Fucking amazing!"
Floyd London (The Almighty – Bass)

"My first Donington experience was when I was a teenager in '81 when it was AC/DC and Whitesnake. Whitesnake were on their 'Come and Get It' album and it was awesome and all the bands that played were excellent. I just remember it so well and it was one of my first festival experiences and I was just hooked."
Pete Spiby **(Black Spiders – Vocals / Guitar)**

"Monsters Of Rock was the highlight of our year. We worked it for 11 years right through the glory days of Whitesnake, Iron Maiden, AC/DC, ZZ Top, Kiss and

Ozzy. All the heavy metal bands that meant anything played Donington...the names are legendary now – Guns N Roses, Metallica, Bon Jovi, David Lee Roth, Dio, Aerosmith, Uriah Heep, Anvil, Motley Crue, Twisted Sister, Wasp... too many to recount. Donington was fun. It was always the same team meeting up at the Priesthouse Hotel under the watchful eye of Maurice Jones. There was a great feeling of camaraderie, we understood the job in hand and even if we never had time to chat on the day, a snatched encounter in catering at most, we'd always have a drink or three back at the hotel later and regale our highlights. I remember one memorable festival where Maurice had had some bad news and wanted to talk, I sat up till 4am just listening, the least I could do for an old friend."

Judy Totton (Monsters Of Rock PR)

"Just 12 months before people were saying it was over for AC/DC after the death of their vocalist Bon Scott but the 'Back In Black' album catapulted AC/DC to worthy headline status. For sheer energy and balls to the wall simple effective rock 'n 'roll they are hard to beat.
One of the surprises on the day was Slade. They were really entertaining and went down a storm."

The Bailey Brothers (Mick & Dez Donington Comperes)

"After a few initial rumours about who was to headline the second festival (Rush, Kiss, Black Sabbath), it

was announced that AC/DC would be the main band with Whitesnake as special guests.

Our entourage more than doubled this year (5 in 1980 to 12 in 1981), including a couple of girlfriends. We travelled down in a transit van. This was to become our normal form of transit for the next decade or so.

For me, the band of the day title was taken from under AC/DC's nose by the mighty blues rock of Whitesnake. Coverdale and co were one of the best live bands around in the early eighties.

AC/DC were let down by over-long gaps between songs. Also, apart from 'THE' Bell, their stage show was a bit sparse. Their shows at later Donington's were much better.

Blue Oyster Cult had a 'very' bad day at the office.

Slade were a breath of fresh air on a wet Saturday afternoon. I can't recall whether it was footballs or toilet rolls (or both) that they threw into the crowd, but I do remember Noddy Holder proclaiming that the rain was 'pissing' in from the (AC/DC)Bell hung from a crane high above the stage. Great fun.

Blackfoot were also in the form of their life in August 1981. 'Good Morning' and 'Wishing Well' going down a storm, but the piece de resistance was 'Highway Song' (a song almost, but not quite as good as Lynryd Skynyrd 'Freebird')."

Paul Hartshorn (Chesterfield)

1982
Status Quo
Gillan, Saxon, Hawkwind, Uriah Heep, Anvil, Tommy Vance

This year was an all British affair with the exception of the Canadian opening act Anvil.
Anvil were heavily influential on the up and coming 'Thrash Metal' scene which has since been covered in great depth in their successful movie 'ANVIL: The Story of Anvil'; Metallica, Anthrax and Slayer all cite Anvil as a big influence on their careers. Not a hugely popular

opener as they were mostly unknown at the time and so had a lot of 'stuff' thrown at them, but would increase in popularity when they were on the bill for the following years Reading Festival.

Two stalwarts of the 'prog rock' scene were also included in the shape of Hawkwind (not a usual MOR band) and Uriah Heep who were gradually evolving into a classic British rock band.

Saxon, now more popular than on their previous appearance, had leap frogged up the bill to sit in the 3rd place slot which in previous years had been held by Scorpions and BOC, both major league players; this showed how Saxon were now contenders. There latest album 'Denim And Leather' included the hits 'Princess of the Night' and 'And The Bands Played On', the latter reaching the top 20 in the UK.

Gillan were in the second place spot this year, now featuring new guitarist Janick Gers (the former White Spirit guitarist) who had replaced Bernie Torme the previous year; Janick Gers is now one of the three guitarists in Iron Maiden and has been since 1990.

Gillan at the time were extremely popular, with Top Of The Pops appearances and chart hit singles, but this was not to last as Ian Gillan (ex Deep Purple vocalist) split the band the same year and left to record the 'Born Again' album with Black Sabbath, who headlined the 'final' Reading Festival in 1983.

Headliners Status Quo were regulars at Reading Festival over the 70's, but this was their only appearance at MOR, perhaps they weren't heavy enough? Quo churned out the hits and the denim and leather clad punters lapped it up and for a change the weather stayed fairly dry.

Third year in a row and still great line-ups, how long could this go on for? A long time as the bill was getting better each year and the amount of 'big' American was due to increase as the festival started to become well known overseas.

Ticket prices had now risen to £10 in advance or £11 on the day and Tommy Vance was still playing records between bands and introducing the acts on the stage.

"Saxon was onstage as we pulled up and it was a mudfest. People were throwing mud and bottles of piss at the stage.
Someone had taught him how to speak to an audience and they finished a number and Biff was saying 'let's calm down, we are Saxon and we don't need all this'. He eventually got them calmed down and he said 'now what we are going to do is our new single and we want you all to go fucking potty' and it all started up all over again. We were 'side-splitting' in our car, watching the entire goings on."
Ian Gillan (Gillan - Vocals)

"The second time we played was great, but not as special as the first one.
A lot of people around the world, we'd just come back from Japan, are interested in the first Donington, especially the younger journalists."
Biff Byford (Saxon -Vocals)

"One year later we were on tour with Rainbow and we were asked to play Donington again and this made Saxon the 'First band to play it TWICE'.

We were in Texas on Thursday with Rainbow, left Friday to fly to UK and arrived Saturday morning in Gatwick, where a private plane took us to East midlands airport. Before we landed the pilot took us over the crowd as the first band was playing. We landed though totally knackered and we were all bronzed with Texas tans.

But the gig was not as good as the first due to a combination of things plus the Quo's crew were very unhelpful to put it politely.

I remember talking to Gary Bardon and Mr Schenker in the drinks tent then we were taken to hotel for an early flight back to the USA and Sunday night we headlined the NY Palladium with Frank Marino as Support; that was a tough schedule for any one but we rose to the challenge and did a great set."

Graham Oliver (Saxon – Guitar)

"The bill for Donington Monsters of Rock in 1982 was Anvil, Uriah Heep, Hawkwind, Saxon, Gillan and Status Quo. Donington for Uriah Heep was fantastic.

We took to the stage after Anvil a Canadian band that were very glam rock and were pelted with mud and abuse so taking to the stage after that reaction we were very unsure of how the audience would react. Also we had not played in the UK for quite a while and thought that we had been forgotten.

We did not need to worry as the roar from the crowd as we took the stage was fantastic. I clearly remember having a small tuning problem with my Les

Paul Guitar and at the end of the show on the crescendo I rubbed the guitar up and down the scaffolding that was holding the P/A and broke off the headstock. I was so high on adrenaline that it did not matter.
It was a brilliant day and one festival that I will always remember from the many we have played over the years."
Mick Box (Uriah Heep – Guitar)

"I have very vivid memories of my first festival!!! It was probably one of the most meaningful yet troubling experiences in my entire career.
Playing first was frightful....to say the least. They were still plugging in speaker cabinets when we began our set. Our live show was very stressful but OK.
My memories or at least the ones I want to have are of the backstage. It was an extravaganza of rock stars, playing there or otherwise. I had the opportunity to have been friends with Howard Johnston from Kerrang! Magazine and he began introducing me to various people to my complete amazement. Some such people were Gary Barden, the ex singer of the Michael Schenker Group, who a week later ended up playing with Michael at the Reading Festival. Other guys like Dee Snider or old acquaintances like the guys from the Diodes an old punk band from Canada. It was very exciting for me.
I remember the photographers came to take pictures of us at our trailer and I distinctly remember our producer Chris Tsangarides and John Sykes being inside the trailer laughing as I was making all kinds of

dog noises as they took the photos of us standing outside the trailer. I also remember some very funny moments as I watched Saxon playing from the VIP section. I noticed Lee Kerslake (Heep drummer) quite buzzed out and a fan asked him for his autograph and he quickly said hold this and he swished his glass of beer all over the guy!!! I was shocked and so was the fan!!! But in the end they were shaking hands and laughing about it.
Another great person I met there was Lord Philip Harvey. He was many of the rock stars personal friends at that time. We ended up doing quite a bit of partying with him during our stay in the U.K. in 82 and 83."

Lips (Anvil – Vocals/Guitar)

"There's a few never forgetting memories from that moment in time.
Ya sure I remember, at like 10..am in the morning being backstage and going out up to the stage to see what it was gonna be all about, only to walk at the side stage area and look first out at the ocean of people and thinking to myself 'Fuck I've never seen so many people up this earlier waiting for a show to start', (there was at that time already over 30.000 head bangers and then turning my eyes towards the stage and being in total shock, being that the stage was totally covered in fresh ripped up grass all over it, and tons of wet mud everywhere on the stage and the backline. And nobody at all was bothering about any of it, to stop it or clean anything. At this moment I thought, this is gonna be more than just another gig. Like, are we even gonna be able to start never mind

finish? It was totally fuck from anything I had ever seen to that point.

Right from the start of the set to the end, there was endless amounts of shit flying non-stop...was simply next to retarded to perform under those conditions, let alone plastic bottles half full with fresh warm just filled urine, being tossed per second spaying anything and everything within it's reach...ya how could anyone forget all that.

Remember though watching and finally getting to see bands like Uriah Heep and Saxon. Was up lifting.....but spent most of the time getting stoned smoking hash and real enjoying getting away from home (Canada).

Robb Reiner (Anvil – Drums)

"We can remember Saxon getting more than a fair share of crap thrown at them on stage.

Vocalist Biff Byford stopped the band playing and said:

"If you don't stop throwing we ain't gonna play anymore, calm down"

Status Quo were always the Monsters of Boogie. If you didn't have a denim waist coat and a pair of white trainers where we lived you weren't a rock fan."

The Bailey Brothers (Mick & Dez Donington Comperes)

"Our job started maybe six months before the event, building up to it and then arranging photo calls and supervising interviews and TV crews on the day. We were fielding requests right up to the last minute with Kerrang! always managing to talk their way into passes for every member of their staff...20 and counting. The thing about Donington was it attracted press from all over the world so we frequently had to put the photographers in relays in the pit. Getting them in was easy, getting them out much harder, particularly if they only had two songs each. My assistant Carmine, who came back to work Donington for me even after she'd left my company, was a dab hand at that. We marched 'em in and we marched 'em out. And there was always the inevitable photographer who just turned up from France with no pass (I'd usually let them shoot the photo calls even if we couldn't give them photo pit access)."

Judy Totton (Monsters Of Rock PR)

"I don't think that 1982 was one of the best years in the history of Donington.
The main problem for the headliners Status Quo was the sound. Rolled down in front of the speaker stacks either side of the stage were two massive reproductions of (I think) the 'Just Supposin' album cover, whether this caused the sound problems I don't know, but none of the other bands on the bill suffered the same fate. After about an hour of 'Quo we decided to make our way home. This was the first of only two times that I left early. Because we only live approx 30 minutes from Donington we even managed to get back to the local for a pint.
Therefore the band of the day was probably Gillan, just edging out Saxon. The highlights of Gillan's set were a new song called 'Bluesy Blue Sea' and a 'new' old song called 'Black Night'. Also I remember

Janick Gers emblazoned all in white climbing up the speakers during his solo spot.
The best of Saxon's set was the song that they had written about their appearance at the 1980 Donington show '….And The Bands Played On'.
The best merchandise of the day was the Uriah Heep red 'Abominog' t-shirts."
Paul Hartshorn (Chesterfield)

1983
Whitesnake
Meat Loaf, ZZ Top, Twisted Sister, Dio, Diamond Head, Tommy Vance

From 1983 the world of rock and metal music sat up and definitely started to take notice of the Monsters Of Rock festival. For the 4th years festival, the line-up included four bands from the USA and two British bands.

This was the second appearance of Whitesnake, but this time they were on the top of the pile; another British band gets to headline Donington and what better than the 'bluesy rock' of Mr

Coverdale and co. The line-up of Whitesnake had changed radically; out were Ian Paice, Bernie Marsden and Neil Murray and their replacements were Cozy Powell, Mel Galley and Colin Hodgkinson.

The Whitesnake video 'Whitesnake Commandos : Donington '83' was released on video the same year, covering most of the headline performance; with a camouflaged theme running from the programme and t-shirts to Cozy wearing a camouflaged t-shirt and Mel Galley in a khaki coloured jumpsuit on the day. A stand out moment was the Cozy Powell drum solo to the '1812 Overture' and '633 Squadron' theme accompanied by helicopters with searchlights and the crying women during 'Ain't No Love In The Heart Of The City'. Whitesnake would be a considerably different breed of band when they made their return in 1990.

Diamond Head were the opening band on the day and the favourites of Lars Ulrich played 'Am I Evil' as their opening track; Metallica would later cover this song and make it a staple of their live shows. Merv Goldsworthy played on bass at this time, prior to leaving to join British AOR legends FM.

One of the most anticipated sets of the day was from Dio. Ronnie James Dio had played in Rainbow and most recently Black Sabbath, before leaving them in 1982. This performance by Dio was one of his first shows with his new band, featuring Jimmy Bain on bass (ex Rainbow), Vivien Campbell on guitar (ex Sweet Savage; after

Dio he joined Whitesnake and is currently in Def Leppard) and Vinnie Appice on drums (ex Black Sabbath, now with Heaven & Hell); basically a rock supergroup in the vein of Rainbow and Whitesnake. The 'Holy Diver' album had just been released and so the set was heavily based around this with a couple of Rainbow and Black Sabbath songs thrown into the mix.

If any band was going to get stuff thrown at them it was Twisted Sister; looking like a bunch of builders dressed in fluorescent clothes and makeup they were an obvious target and get things thrown at them they did. The audience 'lobbed' everything at the band that they could, but they didn't expect the kind of reaction that they got from Dee Snider (lead singer). Dee invited anyone who was throwing stuff to come up on stage for a fight, of course there were no takers and they won the crowd over.

ZZ Top were on a new high, with massive success in the UK with the album 'Eliminator' that had been released that year in March. One of the most popular bands of the day and the first of three appearances at the festival.

Meatloaf came and went and again had a vast amount of items thrown at him; not a popular choice with the metal masses, but a good filler before Whitesnake.

It was quite a sunny day and unlike other Doningtons there was no mud bath! Tommy Vance yet again provided the banter and in between bands music.

"We played in '83 with Cozy and we shot the video for 'Whitesnake Commandos" also with Mel Galley, God bless his soul; God bless both of them. They're all good memories, all positive, playing at home isn't it."
David Coverdale (Whitesnake – Vocals)

"I remember it being a spectacular event and something we were really proud to take part in, especially since it just after the release of our first album so it was a very special time to present it to an audience, especially a British audience, which was very cool.
Having known the guys from Whitesnake for a long time it was nice to see them again of course and it was the first place that I met the guy who would become our drummer for ten years and that was Simon Wright.
It was the first time that I met Simon and he had just gotten the gig with AC/DC, he was only 18 years old at the time and I knew his wife, she came over and introduced me to Simon and I loved him from the off, what a great kid, just the best. Here was a guy who had played with some other bands, but had never really played with anything of that scale and suddenly he was thrust into the fore of one of the biggest bands on the face of the earth. He handled it so well, he was in awe of them, and he was just a regular person, so that was one of the things that I remember the most of Donington.
It was one of our first gigs; I think that we had played a couple of shows before then, I think we had done some small American tour of some kind and then

came over to Britain, so it was our first time in Europe for us.
There was some mud thrown on the first show and it hit a lot of people, but they didn't throw any mud at us and being that we were second on the bill we should have been a good target; those people certainly respected what I had done before with Sabbath and Rainbow, so they gave me the same kind of respect that I always give them."
Ronnie James Dio (Dio – Vocals)

"We came to Donington and now we've had hit records out. Out of 40,000 people, 90% loved us, but 10% of the crowd can throw a lot of shite.
So we were up there and we were getting bottles and shit flying all over the place and we got to a break and I thought I'd call them out again and I said 'YOU MUTHA FUCKERS, MEET ME AT THE SIDE OF THE STAGE', but they had already heard that one at Reading so they went 'YAAAAAAAA!!!!!!'
So we did another song and we were ducking pebbles and bottles.
So, I said 'Have we got any friends here? Do you know what, if I was out there and my friend was onstage and someone was throwing things at him I would BEAT THE PISS OUT OF THAT MUTHA FUCKER?' So I then said 'if you're my friends then kick this Mutha fucker's ass and if he's too big, get a whole bunch of you and bring him down to the ground.'
We started the next song and it was like Altamont with the Rolling Stones, you could see fights all over

the audience. There were people beating people down, awesome!

Meatloaf was on the bill and he was just fuckin' drunk off his ass. I'm not going to get into the conversation that we had, but he passed the 'baton of rock' to me, I didn't ask him for it, but apparently he had it! But, he went out onstage and he was shit faced and he was getting angry at all the shit being thrown. He walked to the edge of the stage and said 'ARE YOU MUTHA FUCKERS THROWING STUFF, C'MON'. They buried that sad fuck!

I saw Meatloaf outlined in litre plastic bottles! I was at the side of the stage and I said 'NO', and he staggered back and the bottles fell to the ground. How drunk have you got to be to tell an English crowd to throw shit at me?"

Dee Snider (Twisted Sister – Vocals)

"We'd already known about Reading and knew that Donington was more of a heavy rock show, so we knew that people who came to see lighter acts wouldn't be pissed off, because there were some heavy bands on the bill, us, ZZ Top, Whitesnake and Meat Loaf, back when he was really popular.

I remember we went over great, the show itself was spectacular, there were about 70,000 people there, and I remember thinking 'wow that was different to Reading'. Everybody loved it and we didn't get anything thrown at us, but Meatloaf?

He said 'Alright, if you think you can throw shit, go for it!' When you tell people to go for it, they threw everything and the kitchen sink at him! Fucking mud pies! They threw toilet paper.

It got so bad at the end of his set that while ZZ Top's road crew were changing over, they were so afraid to come out that they were using cymbals as shields! They were holding the cymbals and they were going 'BING BING BING'.
It was a lot of fun."
Jay Jay French (Twisted Sister – Guitar)

"One funny thing that sticks in my mind was that there were portable bathrooms where there hook them up to a water supply and it looks like a regular bathroom, even though it's on wheels.
The bathroom had about four or five stalls in it and regular urinals, but they were just for people in the bands. There were Dio, ZZ Top, Meatloaf, Whitesnake and us. I was sitting in the bathroom on 'the ole throne' and then I heard someone come in and sit next to me and I said 'who's that next to me?' and he said 'it's Jon Lord' and I was like 'how are you doing?' I was there having a conversation with Jon Lord of Deep Purple on the toilet!! They could probably have sold those stalls for a fortune after the festival, after all the famous bands had come in and dropped a load. So, we finished our conversation and I left, never having even spoke to him face to face. But I actually saw him half hour later and I did say that we'd just had a pretty interesting conversation, which was a very funny thing.
When Meatloaf went on stage, Bob Kulick was playing with him at the time, sporting his bald head, which was way ahead of the times. Meatloaf came on stage and said 'do you wanna throw something' and he was nearly buried in the stuff!

I always remember that Whitesnake headlined and that they had helicopters, I won't forget that! They were definitely making a point that they were headlining."
Eddie Ojeda (Twisted Sister – Guitar/Backing Vocals)

"I don't drink and I don't do drugs, but I still don't remember that much.
We went on during the daylight, which was tough for us as we're used to going on in a dark club or dark hall, to go on in the sunlight it was a bit weird for us.
It was a great show; it was such a good feeling for us, because you don't have 'big shows' like that in the US. It was so new for us and a great feeling. We were up and coming and everyone like us, except for some of those in other bands. They were like 'what are these fuckin' idiots doing?'
It was a phenomenal experience and I remember we stayed for the whole night. I remember seeing ZZ Top and Cozy Powell with Whitesnake and his drum solo with the helicopter; it was a great festival and a lot of fun."
Mark 'The Animal' Mendoza (Twisted Sister – Bass)

"It was a really big deal to us, as it was probably this biggest gig that we had done to that date, about 35,000 people or so we'd been told.
It's always hard opening a show and we'd been told that it was difficult, but we were just glad to get away with not going down badly and getting bottled off.
I do remember Meatloaf getting bottled at that gig.

There was a lot of mud going onto the stage. They were throwing chunks of mud at the band if they didn't like them.

One the things that made it difficult for us was that we had just come out of making our 3rd album 'Canterbury', which had been a difficult album to make. We had introduced a keyboard player and we also had a new drummer and bass player, so we were all still finding our feet. This gig was the first that the keyboard player had done with us, his name was Bob, so that must have been a bit of a shock to him, straight to Donington for you first gig!

Things seemed to go ok but it wasn't our finest; at least we didn't die a death.

I remember briefly meeting people backstage like Whitesnake, but not ZZ Top, they kept themselves to themselves in their portakabin.

I do remember that there was a big argument between Meatloaf and Dee Snider and they came into our dressing room so that they could have the argument. There was a big row and I think that they wanted to keep out of the way of their band members, so that they could let off steam at each other and that was quite interesting to hear the two of them, two scary Americans going at each other, face to face.

I did get nervous going to the gig, I can remember someone drove us there and each time you saw signs for Donington, my heart would go as we were getting closer. It's not far from where I live, it's probably only an hour or an hour and a halfs drive. We had to leave at some ridiculous time as we were

first on at one o'clock in the afternoon, so we were told that we needed to be there for eleven.
I just remember it being a nerve wracking gig and I was worried about how we would be received and I think someone had organised, through the fan club, a banner competition. If you designed your banner and we picked the best one, you'd win a signed album. So there was maybe a dozen big banners in the audience with Diamond Head on and the logo and that was quite exciting to look at and see the support."
Brian Tatler (Diamond Head – Guitar)

"I did Donington with AC/DC and Twisted Sister.
It was a remarkable festival and a great place to play at, always great promoters."
Phil Carson (Ex head of Atlantic records)

"The following year I was a guest and I will never forget I was talking to David Coverdale and Ian Paice when a drunk barged in to hospitality area and shouted to David 'Is it true Tommy Bolin was a Junkie?' Now Tommy was David's close friend and band mate who tragically died at a young age and David went white with fury and I had to restrain him before he took the guys head off and security dragged the asshole away."
Graham Oliver (Saxon – Guitar)

"I also went to the Whitesnake headliner show with ZZ Top, I remember being slightly disappointed that Whitesnake played most of the same set I had played with Ian Paice and Neil Murray when the original

band folded, but it was a good show and the crowd loved it, and they are the important people at all festivals."
Bernie Marsden (Whitesnake – Guitar)

"I went to Donington to '83 in response to the Dio 'Holy Diver' album coming out. It was Diamond Head, Dio, Twisted Sister, Meatloaf, ZZ Top and Whitesnake. The weird thing was that we ended up touring with ZZ Top."
Toby Jepson (Little Angels - Vocals)

"Twisted Sister didn't come to the Monsters of Rock to be taken seriously AND THEY WEREN'T!"
The Bailey Brothers (Mick & Dez Donington Comperes)

"From what had been a relatively disappointing year (1982), we now came to a year that I still recall as one of the best days ever…topped off by a magnificent version of 'Mistreated' by Whitesnake………when Coverdale announced that this would 'probably be the last time he would ever play this song' you just knew it was gonna be something special. In fact the overall Whitesnake performance is still my favourite of all the headlining acts over the years. 'Here I go again' was also brilliant, especially Coverdale's singing at the start. Visually the highlight was Cozy Powell's drum solo, which now incorporated the '633 Squadron' music as well as the '1812 Overture'. During the '633 Squadron' section the festival site was 'dive-bombed' by light aircraft (helicopters I think). There was over

£50,000 worth of pyrotechnics used during the Whitesnake set. Magnificent.

But Whitesnake were not the only band on form on the day.

ZZ Top were riding on the back of their 'Eliminator' album and received favourable comments all round. One memory I have of their set was when a naked female started dancing to 'Gimme All Your Lovin' just in front of our base camp. This performance was supported by appreciative jeering from all the males in the vicinity.

Twisted Sister's Dee Snider probably gave the best introduction to a song ever at Donington………. "This next song's a bit slow for Twisted Sister……but its f*****g mean". The song in question was 'Destroyer' from their 'Under The Blade' album.

Apart from Whitesnake, my other favourite band of the day was DIO. The band was playing their very first ever live show (apart from a couple of warm-ups). The soon to be classic album 'Holy Diver' had just been released. Their set included a mixture of songs from this album plus various Rainbow and Black Sabbath classics including 'Stargazer', 'Heaven and Hell' etc.

The biggest disappointment of the day was Diamond Head. I had expected them to perform better than they did.

I remember the weather being good this year."

Paul Hartshorn (Chesterfield)

1984
AC/DC

Van Halen, Ozzy Osbourne, Gary Moore, Y&T, Accept, Motley Crue, Tommy Vance

Back for its 5th Anniversary and for what most fans have agreed was the best line-up of all of the Monsters Of Rock Festivals from 1980 to 1996.

With AC/DC back for their 2nd headline appearance at the festival, you couldn't want for a more popular band to be topping the bill.
With the 'Flick Of The Switch' album released the year before, AC/DC slotted 'Guns For Hire' and the title track into the set alongside many favourites, now all considered classics; for the encore of 'For Those About To Rock' there was the accompaniment of the now famous cannons.
Special guests on the day didn't come any bigger than Van Halen. Massive in the USA and making a rare UK appearance, British fans were treated to a selection of greatest hits and some from their latest album, the record breaking '1984'; the last to feature David Lee Roth who left shortly after to be replaced by Sammy Hagar. Songs played on the day from '1984' included 'Panama', 'Hot For Teacher', 'House Of Pain' and the song that Van Halen are internationally recognised for 'Jump'.
DLR high kicked his way through the performance and told 'tall tales' between songs, Eddie Van Halen played the most intricate and complicated guitar seen at Donington so far, Alex Van Halen playing the largest drum kit in Donington history and Michael Anthony, well he played solid and perfunctory bass.
Also on the bill was Ozzy Osbourne whose band at the time featured another guitar legend, Jake E. Lee; Lee was a former member of Mickey Ratt which went on to become the platinum selling Ratt, he was also an early member of Dio. Lee was the permanent replacement for Randy Rhoads who had died in tragic plane crash with

Ozzy's tour bus; Brad Gillis of Night Ranger had played with Ozzy but was not considered a permanent member.

Gary Moore played his way through a short blues / metal package and showed his guitar skills to all; his set was incredibly loud.

Y&T from the USA and Accept were also appearing on the day, but most people and press were in attendance to see the UK debut of Motley Crue. Having just released the 'Shout At The Devil' album, the Crue were starting to make a name for themselves and not just for their music. Known for the wild times and wild hair, Motley Crue's performance on the day was short, but drew a massive crowd; this would be the first of their four performances to date at Donington.

For the first time in MOR history, there were bars selling actual alcohol inside the venue!!! The annoying problem for most people was that the bars were only open for usual British bar times, these being 11:30am to 2pm and then re-opening from 6pm to 9pm, bizarre compared to the alcohol on sale at Download now, from open to close. You were still able to bring in your own alcohol if dispensed into the appropriate containers.

Highlights of the show and interviews were also featured on BBC2 on 'The Old Grey Whistle Test'.

"It was us Van Halen, Y&T, Accept and more and it was just incredible and it was the biggest show that I had played up until then and to play it in England with all my family and there!

There was the 'bigness' of the set, the production, all that was going on and the trucks and the buses and everything, my family were all blown away.

They remember me just bashing my drums in my bedroom and then suddenly I'm playing in front of 80,000 people. That was definitely my best moment so far; there have been others, but that was England and it stood out as being really important.

Simon Wright (AC/DC – Drums)

"We consider ourselves fortunate to have played probably the best Monsters of Rock lineup in the history of the festival. Still to this day people tell us that Castle Donington MOR 1984 was the best lineup the festival ever had. Every band on that bill we were either good friends with or had played shows with. It was cool to see them all and experience such a monumental day together.

Of course one thing that will never escape my memories of that show was being bombarded by the punters throwing bottles of piss on stage. When we'd previously supported AC/DC on tour for two months, they warned us that every band who opens for AC/DC gets stuff thrown at them and gets booed off the stage. The AC/DC band and crew were shocked when audiences everywhere never once threw anything at Y&T, but in actual fact, gave us encores almost every night. Same with The Reading festival; heard we would be pelted - never happened. We knew it was the norm for that to happen, but having bottles of piss hit my guitar and splatter up on my body while performing was a real downer. Yeah, we realized they did that with every band, but it sucked

anyway and makes you feel like a moving target."
Dave Meniketti (Y&T – Guitar / Vocals)

"I remember our bus driver told Castle Donington security that he had AC/DC in the bus. So Y&T got escorted by police motorcade through the festival grounds to backstage. We felt rather important for a few minutes there.   Don't get me started on the piss bottles! I was so angry after our set that I punched out the window in our dressing room. But, when I think back to the ridiculous clothes we were wearing that day--I guess we deserved it.   Motley Crue was staying at our hotel, hanging in the bar. The first thing Tommy Lee said was, "Where can I get some flesh." I said, "Good luck, dude, we're in England...The punters here are all dudes". We knew all the bands on the bill that day and it was great fun to catch up with everyone backstage. But AC/DC was the only band that didn't fraternize; they stayed cloistered in their little dressing room trailer. So I barged in and said hello to all of them before they went on stage. All the other bands were fired up and partying, but these guys just sat there as if they were about to go to the gas chamber. It was strange. Maybe they feared the piss bottles!"   **Phil Kennemore (Y&T – Bass)**

"I will never forget when we played the "Monsters Of Rock" festival at Donington back in 1984. We just came back from a very long U.S. tour and it was our first concert in Europe after having the worldwide success with the

"Balls To The Wall" album. And the success stayed on.
We were the second band on stage but the reception was that of at least a co-headliner. Everybody was singing along every song we played and so that festival (together with the other two "Monsters Of Rock" festivals in Germany that same year) became our breakthrough in Europe.
But there were strange things happening as well. During the gig we saw something big flying onto the stage and when we looked closer, it was a horse head (a real one - believe me). Also, somebody threw an apple on stage which hit Wolf's guitar so hard, that the neck pick-up was shot through the guitar's backside.
But hey - that's rock'n'roll - and I still have great memories about the gig in Donington."
Stefan Kaufmann (Accept – Drums)

"Saw Eddie Van Halen, standing with Gary Moore on the side of the stage, Gary was in shock, Eddie was just about the best at the time I think! Met Dave Lee Roth and Steve Vai for the first time at Donington." **Bernie Marsden (Whitesnake – Guitar)**

"I remember going to the '84 one, especially to see Van Halen. I remember shaking hands backstage with Eddie Van Halen who was one of my heroes."
Brian Tatler (Diamond Head – Guitar)

"The first one I went to was AC/DC, Van Halen & Ozzy Osbourne.
I was lucky enough to have a backstage pass and met Eddie Van Halen & Jake E Lee, my absolute hero at the time."
Myke Gray (Skin – Guitar)

"Seeing Van Halen with Diamond Dave Lee Roth again should have been the ultimate experience but Dave seemed to think we gave a toss about his experience with a tart in a hotel room that must have took him 5 minutes to tell the story.
Then we get the obligatory drum and bass solo.
Ok, Eddie's piece was worth witnessing in the flesh, but add up the waffle and all the solos and we could have had another shit load of songs.
It turned out to be their final show with DLR and as huge VH fans we just wanted to hear the songs."
The Bailey Brothers (Mick & Dez Donington Comperes)

"My first Monsters of Rock was 1984, AC/DC and Van Halen; I joined MCP that year."
Stuart Galbraith (ex – Donington Organiser)

"We had our own portakabin in the guest area which became a bit of a haven for many of the snappers. We also had our regular local press turn up year in year out, many bringing us little presents; it was like a Christmas club. I remember Maurice being horrified one year to find we'd been burning incense to create a chill out factor – he didn't think it was heavy enough at all. The local media were always

very supportive and there was a tradition in the early days of as many of the acts as possible going into Radio Trent on the Friday night to record a round table. Even the headliners would take part if they could. That just wouldn't happen now. It was hosted by a DJ called Graham (who came to a very sad end)."
Judy Totton (Monsters Of Rock PR

"This was my first year and it featured an absolute barnstormer of a lineup (many, myself included consider this the best MOR lineup). I travelled down via a concert coach company with 1 friend who I managed to lose within 45 minutes of entering the arena.

On entering the arena I was absolutely struck dumb by the sheer size of the crowd, the arena and the monster of a stage. As we positioned ourselves stage left Motley Crue hit the stage, they performed a quick energetic set and managed to dodge most of the missiles heading their way, the throwing of empty and piss filled bottles was already a tradition and the openers usually got more than their fair share purely for being the first band up. Next up were German band Accept who seemed to fair better on the bottle front and also seemed to go down reasonably well, however, I was never a fan of Udo's squawking vocals so I spent most of their set drinking and chatting to some Italians in front of us. After a short break Y&T were up; this was the first band of the day that I really wanted to see and they did not disappoint, I surged forward and secured a decent spot to headbang my way through their set, frantically during the fantastic 'Forever'. If I remember correctly some bloke dressed as the robot from the cover of their latest album 'In Rock We Trust' wondered onto the stage at one point. From then on the day got better and better, next up was Gary Moore, who at the time was doing really well over here and had several hits that were circulating the airwaves, he played like the true axe hero he was, however, I cannot for the life of me remember who else was in his band at the time or what the set list consisted of, I think that the beer was starting to take hold of my senses. Four bands in and a bladder full of beer and it was time to experience my first festival toilets, they did not disappoint and were as dirty and smelly as I had been reliably informed they would be. On the way back into the crowd it was noticeable that the mixture of sun and alcohol was having an effect on many as there were scores of people who were sleeping/ passed out littering the grass near the back, to this day, this is something that has never changed, some people do not seem to manage past the first band before they adopt this position and are then usually covered in crap from their friends or drawn/ painted on.

Near the front the crowd was starting to condense as Ozzy hit the stage, he stormed through an impressive rat arsed set which concluded with him emotionally receiving a gold disk on stage from the late, great Tommy Vance for his latest album 'Bark At The Moon'.

Next up were special guests Van Halen who I would witness four more times in the future but they were *never as good as they were on this day in their original lineup. I stormed to the front and went berserk whilst they played hit after hit from their back catalogue and the current masterpiece '1984' which of course included the rather radio friendly 'Jump'. At one point David Lee Roth informed us that he was going to buy us all a beer; he was always a master of bullshit but I do not know whether or not anyone tried it on at the bar, I had visions of scores of people queued up requesting a beer on Dave's tab, I could imagine the response that they would get from the staff! By this time the bottle fights had reached fever pitch, but it was now not just bottles being slung about it was anything loose, I just managed to dodge a hail of half full yoghurt pots, all of which hit the bloke in front of me, he was absolutely covered but too pissed by then to actually care.*

Van Halen finished and it took me some considerable time to get out of the crowd for another trek to the submerged latrines, it was my first time in such a dense crowd and I must admit, I got a wee bit panicky trying to push my way through the masses. At the back of the arena a strange naked cricket match was going on? The rules did not appear to follow the game to the letter but at least ten merry revellers were having fun participating, I wondered if 'cock before wicket' would be considered as out? As dusk descended it was not long before that day's headliner- the mighty AC/DC burst on to the stage surrounded by masses of lights and easily that day's best and loudest sound. I was transfixed by Angus and his continual motion and boundless energy, from the second they hit the stage he just kept going and did not stop till the end. I was not the greatest fan of their recorded material at that time but they won me over big time that night, amongst my favourite tunes they played were 'Highway to Hell', 'Whole Lotta Rosie', 'Back In Black', 'Hells Bells' (complete with full size bell being twatted by Brian J), 'T.N.T.' and 'For Those About to Rock' (complete with canon firing finale). For my first time experiencing a festival headline set DC definitely lived up to my expectations.

And that was it, after a rather cool firework display the show was over and it was time to find the blasted coach, which took ages mainly because several hundred other coaches had arrived after us so it was like finding a needle in a haystack. Still, about 50 mins later I was re-united with the coach and friend that I had lost at the beginning of the show, he never went again, I don't think he got on with the sheer size of the crowd, however, that was the beginning of my love affair with Donington Park, one that continues to this day."
Roger Moore (Glinton, Peterborough)

"What a scorcher…….the weather was red hot. I even got sunburn.
The day's line up wasn't too bad either. Most people would probably look back on the 1984 show as having the best line up of all.
AC/DC performed much better than in 1981 and rolled out the cannons for the Donington crowd for the first time. 'For Those About To Rock' was

televised on 'The Old Grey Whistle Test' a few weeks later.

I wasn't a big Van Halen fan prior to the event, but I got carried away with all the hype and decided to give them a closer look. Venturing down to the front for the first time in 5 years. I really enjoyed their set....even Michael Anthony's bass solo (he rolled around the stage with his bass clutched to his chest if my memory serves me well). When I made my way back up to the rest of our troupe they all said that they had been disappointed with Van Halen. Maybe the performance didn't carry too well towards the back of the crowd, but from my vantage point (approx 6 rows from the front) they were very good.

I remember Ozzy performing with his usual 'craziness' and also receiving a Gold Disc during his set.

I recall Gary Moore resurrecting 'Parisienne Walkways' for the day (I think he had previously dropped the song from his usual set list). His set comprised of the usual mixture of rockers and ballads.

I enjoyed Y&T. I still like to give their 'Meanstreak' album a spin every once in a while.

Neither Motley Crue nor Accept ever really did anything for me, although I do remember a big surge to the front when Motley Crue came on stage about half hour earlier than advertised.

The event T-shirt had pictures of gravestones on the back, each one showing the line up from previous Doningtons....a neat idea I thought (I still have mine, in fact I still have all the event T-shirts and programmes)."

Paul Hartshorn (Chesterfield)

1985
ZZ Top
Marillion, Bon Jovi, Metallica, Ratt, Magnum, Tommy Vance

The bill this year was a bill of two halves. Three bands making their debut and only Donington performances and three bands who would return again, two in headline slots.

Openers Magnum were at the time unsigned, but they were head hunted by a talent scout from the Polydor labels German office. Having just released 'On A Story Tellers Night' in the UK on

FM Records, Polydor had picked up on this and come to watch their performance at Donington, signing them in the backstage area.

Next up were Ratt; raised in LA like Motley Crue and of the similar 'hair metal' contingent which included Poison, who were yet to make their Donington debut. Ratt were already big news in the States with 'Round And Round' already an MTV hit. Lead guitarist Robbin Crosby sadly died from AIDS in 2002 at the age of 42; his guitar dexterity on the day was very popular.

Marillion made their only appearance at MOR in the special guest spot on the day, which seemed a little out of place for a 'prog rock' band at a rock and metal festival; although an exceptional band, could they have been described as a 'Monster of Rock'. At the time Marillion were riding high on the success of their chart singles 'Garden Party', 'Punch and Judy', 'Assassing' and their biggest hit then and which they haven't topped since, the passionate, yet heart-rending, 'Kayleigh'.

Bon Jovi were making their debut at Donington, only to return 2 years later as triumphant headliners. Their album '7800° Fahrenheit' had been released four months before and so was already a favourite with their adoring fans; tracks included from it on the day featured were 'Only Lonely', 'In And Out Of Love' and the rousing 'Tokyo Road' as their opener.

Making their first appearance, the band with the record for the most shows at Donington were Metallica. Playing mid afternoon with original bass player Cliff Burton, they were like nothing else at the festival and were more fitting with Download Festival now; Burton was die in a coach crash only 13 months later in Sweden on the 'Master Of Puppets' tour.

Metallica were targets for bottles on the day, but were targets for adoration from that point on; their first headline show at MOR was in 1995, but they also played in '87 & '91, rising up the bill each time.

ZZ Top were 'topping' the bill this year and would not return until 2009, then in the 3rd place slot.

Playing a greatest hits set, packed full of tracks from 'Eliminator' and their illustrious back catalogue. ZZ Top would release their 10th album 'Afterburner' 2 months later, but surprisingly no tracks from the album were played on the day. What did make an appearance was the ZZ Top car, the red 1933 Ford 3-window coupé Hot Rod from their videos, suspended above the crowd from a helicopter.

Great sunny weather for the whole festival and the dulcet tones of Tommy Vance again throughout the day.

"Growing up as a fan of music and metal, clutching my copies of Sounds and Kerrang! on a weekly basis, as I grew up through the eighties, getting to see Metallica's name on a Donington poster in 1985 was obviously a pretty big deal. We were bright eyed and completely star struck and we were so psyched to come in there and be a part of that whole thing.

We went on that first year early in the afternoon; this was back then and whenever we played festivals it would always be with rental gear and half the issues were 'would the gear function?' We wouldn't get to the gear until we were actually at the site, so you never really knew what you were walking into.

It was early in the afternoon and we were ready to go out there and just throwdown as hard as we could. The main memory and the story that has become folklore from that gig was that there was a pigs head thrown up onto the stage. We were playing and it was back in the day when there was a lot of mud throwing, bottles of piss and all that type of stuff, which we had been warned about and took no offence to, as it was all part of the fun and games; but when the old pigs head ended up on stage, I remember the look on Cliff Burton's face was one of surprise and 'that they really go a step further here!' It's all true!!

It was a fun day and our first foray into British 'mega festivals'. It was certainly the first time that anybody playing our type of music was introduced to an audience that was that big and varied in it's make up.

It was a very varied line-up and we were obviously proud to represent, the kind of music that we were representing and it certainly was the first time that an audience of that kind of cross section of rock fans, were introduced to us, or a band of our ilk.

We must have made some impact because I remember I saw Marillion about a month later, they were playing in Copenhagen where we were recording 'Master Of Puppets' and I went to see them as I was quite a big Marillion fan actually. I remember at one point Fish was talking and introducing the band, with a bit of stage banter. All of a sudden he started talking about 'we're not like some of these new bands that you run into at the festivals playing this horrible noisy stuff' and then Marillion, lo and behold, went into their attempt at 30 seconds of 'speed metal'. I'm not sure if they were aware that I was in the audience, but it was quite funny and there was a smile on my little Danish face because we must have made some kind of impact on the other bands.

The festival was certainly a fun day and there was a great 'piss up' back at the hotel that was a couple of miles from the site where a bunch of the other bands were playing. Some of the guys from Ratt were hanging out and some of the guys from Venom came up and we had a lot of fun."

Lars Ulrich (Metallica – Drums)

"It was a really hot typical summer's afternoon and Donington was quite a day in the History of Marillion. It was one of those occasions that put us in books as being a good festival band. We played just before ZZ Top and really rocked the audience so much so that when the ZZ Top car was flown over the stadium I don't think that many of the crowed actually saw it and realised the significance of (ZZ Top arriving).

We didn't get to see ZZ Top as they had their own enclosure inside the enclosure INSIDE the back stage area. My guess is they were not wanting to be disturbed.

We were in the band area which was pretty secure with Bon Jovi and the others. I don't remember much

socializing going on except with the Magnum boys as we new them quite well and they were and still are good blokes I imagine although I haven't seen any of them for years.
Bon Jovi looked the part and played a good set as far as I remember, but we were more focussed on our own show than anything else My Wife Fiona was there with me and enjoyed herself along with the other Wags.
Interestingly we played just before Bon Jovi at Rock In Rio back in the early 90's and they put their heads round the door and wished us good luck having remembered us from those earlier years."
Pete Trewavas (Marillion – Bass)

"To be Honest I was trippin' a little before we played because I was on the sides of the stage watching the other bands play before our set and I was seeing plastic one gallon milk jugs full of piss being chucked up at the stage and all over each other in the crowd.
And I was thinking, if I get hit in the fucking head with a jug of piss I'm gonna lose it.
What did come flying onstage was even more shocking, some stooge cut the head off a pig and threw the head on stage......Ummm, was that 1985? Ummm no it was 1578 that's right!!
Unbelievable gigs there. I had heard that while Ozzy was on that another part of the pig flew up there and all they could tell was that it was a female....
Hello Cleveland!"
Bobby Blotzer (Ratt – Drums)

"We had a German record executive, come over from Germany; he had approached us and had heard the 'On A Storytellers Night' album. A DJ gave him the album and said to him 'you should sign this band'; he then contacted us and said that he wanted to put the album out on the Polydor label, who he worked for.
So I can remember that we went on stage at Donington and I turned around and I could see this German guy, he was called Michael Göhler and he had come to see us play live.
So we played, I don't remember much about the playing part, but our manager then came up to us backstage and said that Michael wanted to sign us to Polydor. That was obviously the start of things for the band; he signed us and helped us a lot over the years.
I watched ZZ Top and I watched Marillion from out front. I remember also being interviewed in a caravan with a guy from Ratt; but I didn't even remember seeing Metallica, they were in their infancy then. I can remember Jon Bon Jovi walking around, but I didn't actually see them play."
Tony Clarkin (Magnum – Guitar)

"That was the day that we signed a major deal with Polydor, a lovely German guy called Michael **Göhler** and he loved us so much that he got us to sign on the dotted line.
Only a few things were thrown, so we were very lucky."
Bob Catley (Magnum – Vocals)

"I remember that we had to stop on the motorway on the way there for the police to form a cavalcade and escort us in there. I do remember a piece of mud hit my mixing desk, I'd love to thank the guy who did that."
Mark Stanway (Magnum – Keyboards)

"My first great experience at Donington was the first time I ever went. I was watching Ratt play and a mysterious and very cute girl stood beside me and asked which member of Ratt was my favourite. Knowing nothing about Ratt I chose the guitarist who looked like Joe Perry, whereupon she called me a star and gave me a blowjob. My first groupie and the best blowjob I ever got. All thanks to a rather dreadful hair metal band from Los Angeles."
Ginger (The Wildhearts – Vocals/Guitar)

"I went in '85 and Metallica were 'fucking awesome'; although at that time I was a proper 'Ratt head'. I was into all those bands from LA like Ratt and Motley Crue."
Pete Spiby **(Black Spiders – Vocals / Guitar)**

"ZZ Top thought flying their car over Donington would be impressive.
We saw Pink Floyd at Main Road Manchester. During the show a man in a hospital bed appeared on a large video screen above the band on stage. He took off through the ward and out of a window, seconds later a full size bed flow over the length of the football ground with a man in it and crashed right into the video screen.

Now that's impressive!"
The Bailey Brothers (Mick & Dez Donington Comperes)

"I first became aware of some... thing called "Monsters Of Rock" around 83/84. I wasn't really into metal at the time - I was more hard rock (Queen, Magnum, and ZZ Top) and prog (Genesis, Jethro Tull, Marillion) then, so didn't really bother much with the likes of Ozzy, AC/DC, The Scorpions, Motorhead etc. But I'd seen the t-shirts at gigs and the posters in HMV & Kerrang!

In 85 ZZ Top, Marillion & Magnum were all on the bill for that years event. I'd attended my first festival - the infamous 1984 Nostel Priory festival - already and felt ready at the age of 18 for more. There was a company in Leeds called "Cavendish Travel" who did travel & tickets to events all over the country so my girlfriend of the time and myself went to their seedy little office, handed over the money (£12.50 I think, and about a tenner for the coach) and retreated tickets in hand.

The night before, I listened to the Friday Rock Show as DJ Tommy Vance was doing a run down of the bands on the bill that year. Three of the bands I knew well, but Ratt, Metallica and Bon Jovi were very much unknowns at the time. I wasn't impressed with the Metallica track they played – 'Seek And Destroy' How cheesey. But the other two seemed ok.

Saturday morning dawned, and we headed into Leeds to catch the coach. The tannoy system announced the bay to go to catch the bus to the "Donington Pop Concert" and we tutted at National

Express's ignorance of musical genres (as you tended to do at that age). The journey down the M1 was uneventful, but when we pulled off at the last services before getting there (Toddington) there seemed to be long hair and denim everywhere. It started getting exciting.

Getting off the coach into a sea of patches, studs, leather and denim we were swept along to the entrance with a very palpable buzz. Through the gate and into the arena. That's when the "Donington moment" hit me. A sea of every kind of rocker and metalhead you can imagine. The Dunlop Bridge to one side, burger vans and a bar to the other and an incline down to the stage which towered over everything. Nostell Priory was a sedate afternoon at a village fete in comparison.

It seemed a heaving mass of people. Bottles (some empty, some not) seemed to orbit over our heads. I remember one time, later in the day when I'd managed to force my way as far as the sound desk a bottle landing on my back, wedged between me and some guy behind me and glugging its contents down the back of my German army jacket. I never wanted to know what was inside.

To start with we found a spot where we could enjoy the distant site of Magnum (no screens that year I seem to remember) rattle off what seemed to be a very brief 30 minute set.

Ratt were quite a disappointment from that distance, but Metallica were quite a revelation. Far from being the clichéd meathead fodder I was expecting, I found myself getting into their energy.

Bon Jovi showed all the promise they'd later come to

fulfill - ready for the Arena stage, Jon Bon Jovi climbing the speaker stacks.

About this time we started to press forward as my favorite band - Marillion - were about to come on. They were pretty big at the time and really not a Monsters Of Rock type of band but as always they blew me away. It was the first time I'd seen Fish perform without his trademark makeup. There's a picture of Fish kneeling on the stage in Mick Walls "Market Square Heroes" Biography and my face is clearly visible in the crowd.

Then came the wait for the headliners. I moved out of the crush a bit at this stage, and the crowd roared in appreciation as the ZZ Top "Eliminator" car was flown suspended from a helicopter over the crowd - not something you'd get away with now! Their set was fairly unremarkable and a retread of the one I'd seen a couple of years earlier, so the day ended on a bit of an anticlimax. Spirits were high on the way home but I little realised the impact that day had had on me.

As I said earlier, I wasn't much into metal then. But I think that day changed me. I particularly think Metallica changed me. It didn't happen overnight, and it was a few years till I returned but it was to be another major day in my life."

Phil Hull (Download Forum Administrator)

"The first concert I went to was Monsters of Rock 1985.
The sun blazed down all day, the beer was wet and the burgers luke warm, but the music...well, that was a feast to behold!
Bon Jovi had just released 'Slippery When Wet' and

their set was full of sing along songs EVERYONE knew.

Metallica were a relatively unheard of band at the time but after that day and the performance they gave it was obvious to everyone they were going to be BIG! Sorry, did I say big... I meant ABSOLUTELY FUCKIN HUGE!!

To top the day off the 'Eliminator' car was suspended beneath a helicopter and flown over the stage prior to ZZ Top Rockin the Castle!

So, a 250 mile drive home after my first festival with the sights and sounds still buzzing my senses. Only 364 days to go till I get to do it again...Hell Yeah

This year will be my 8th visit to the sacred home of Rock and 25 years since my first and for the 4th year my wife and kids will be with me...and my parents said I'd grow out of it!!!"

Doug Rae (Hawick, Scotland)

"Although on paper the line up looked relatively weak compared to the previous two years, some of the performances were excellent.

ZZ Top had returned to headline this year. Earlier in the (sunny) day their 'Eliminator' car had been flown over the site suspended beneath a helicopter. Several thousand plastic bottles being propelled skywards was quite a sight. The played a good solid headlining set.

I didn't really get Marillion at the time, but like me the previous year, some of the gang went down to the front and came back raving about the performance (most reviews backed this up over the following days….shows how much I know).
Bon Jovi were a fairly new name at the time, their meteoric rise to mega stardom was still a year away. Their performance was brilliant. One member of our gang (a Donington virgin at the time) even predicted that this band would headline within two years…….how right they were.
Definitely a contender for band of the day.
It would take me another 5 or 6 years before I took any notice of Metallica (or any thrash style bands), so it would be unfair for me to pass comment at this stage.
Magnum on the other hand was a band I was looking forward to seeing. The album 'On a Storyteller's Night' was one of my favourites at the time. Even though they were first band on they didn't disappoint. It would another 5 years before a band would challenge them for the title of best opening band. One image I remember is Bob Catley being hit in the crotch with a clump of (accurately thrown) mud. He was wearing very pale jeans which made it stand out even more.
Another warm day."
Paul Hartshorn (Chesterfield)

1986
Ozzy Osbourne

Scorpions, Def Leppard, Motorhead, Bad News, Warlock, Tommy Vance

The rain was back and so was another 'Monsters Of Rock', now into its 7th year and increasing in status each year.

Warlock were up first, fronted by the current poster girl for the 'rock & metal brigade', Dorothy Pesch; at the time she could barely speak any English at the time, but that didn't hinder her and her band from getting the show off to a fine start.

Next on was the controversial choice of the day Bad News. A comedy band formed from the actors in 'The Young Ones' (Mayall, Planer, Edmondson and Richardson), the whole show was filmed to be used as part of the 'Comic Strip Presents' series, entitled 'More Bad News'. Bad News were seen by most of the crowd as a waste of bill space that could have been given to a 'real' band.

Motorhead made their debut at the festival and Lemmy stopped the show when someone fired a rocket at the stage, but carried on again after no one took up his offer to come on stage for a fight; Motorhead are booked in 2010 for their 4th appearance.

There can be only one reason that Donington 1986 sticks in people's memories and that was because of the victorious return to live performance of Rick Allen the drummer with Def Leppard. Allen had been in a severe car crash where his left arm had been torn off on New Years Eve in 1984. Now able to drum one handed, with a specially adapted kit which could involve more footwork, he returned to playing (after a few warm up shows) at probably one of the biggest shows that Def Leppard had done at the time.

Def Leppard received great applause and Rick Allen achieved a standing ovation.

Scorpions were back for their 2nd appearance, six years after their first one and the second German band on the bill for the day. Scorpions were at the high point of their career at the time and were well justified in their 'special guest' slot.

'Love At First Sting' in 1984 had seen them reach #6 in the USA and #17 in the UK and tracks from the album featured heavily in the set including 'Bad Boys Running Wild', 'Big City Nights' and the crowd pleaser 'Rock You Like A Hurricane'.

The 4th British headliner came in the shape of Ozzy Osbourne, back after a two year absence and now looking very much part of the 'hair metal' revolution that was taking place at the time in the UK and especially America. Lowered to the stage on a flamboyant golden throne, Ozzy was certainly perceived as the 'Prince of Darkness'.

Wearing what looked like a diamante dressing gown, Ozzy belted out the hits and several new tracks from his latest album 'Ultimate Sin' including the single 'Shot In The Dark', which summed up the style of the whole album.

So, another festival ended and so did the appearances by Tommy Vance. Sadly no more Thomas 'The' Vance at Donington, apparently due to some article that he had written. So another British institution was gone and the following year Donington would see another

radical change, no British bands and a bill that was known as 'The American Year'.

"We came back for another show in 1986 with Ozzy and Def Leppard.
Looking back, those shows were among the most exciting and unforgettable gigs in the 80's. Donington Rocks!"
Scorpions

"My first experience of Donington was in '86; it was Rick Allen our drummers first big gig after his awful accident where he lost his arm. We had done 'warm ups' where we'd been playing in Ballybunion and other places in Ireland in the middle of nowhere. We had two drummers out; we had Rick Allen and just to play it safe, as he was playing electronic drums which were quite new back then, we had another drummer Jeff Rich, but he couldn't make one of the shows, so Rick played and he was great.
So we got to Donington and it was really emotional, because it was England. We'd never really been accepted as a major band in England, I think because we had such huge success in America and everyone got a little bit pissed off for whatever reasons. But they loved it because Rick had overcome his accident and it was amazing. It was a big deal, for us that one minute he had two arms and we take all that for granted and then he came back and it was huge, as he was doing such an unusual thing, playing drums in a rock band, but now you can't even hear a difference. Back then he was still

learning and learning how to be a person again, which was really cool.
It kind of overshadowed everything and I remember Joe introducing Rick; everyone stood up and it was really emotional, there were people crying, but it worked out.
I also remember the weather wasn't great."
Phil Collen (Def Leppard – Guitar)

"It was the biggest gig we'd ever done and was about 100,000 people.
When we went up the stairs to the stage, I could hardly walk as my knees were shaking and it was so overwhelming. I remember the fans were going crazy and they were very supportive. The fans were so good to us and there was such a good atmosphere.
My heart was beating; I thought I was going to have a heart attack as my adrenalin was so high!
We didn't have a long set, but we gave it our all and I was the first female to play on that stage!
The catwalk out to the people in the crowd was so long and I was so happy.
It was also the first time that I talked to Lemmy and he said 'hey let's go and see Ozzy Osborne', I said to him that I didn't have the right pass. Then someone was walking towards us and he said 'excuse me' and ripped the pass off the guy. He said 'that's mine' and he replied 'it's hers now' and we then walked arm in arm to watch Ozzy Osborne.
I couldn't speak English back then, so our conversations were a little limited.

I watched every band on the day and it was the first time that I got to see the Scorpions, even though I'm from Germany!

Everyone was so proud of Def Leppard's drummer as it was his first gig since his accident and they were amazing.

Somebody threw a firecracker at Motorhead and Lemmy was so pissed off that he walked off stage and then came back and said that if anyone did that again, they wouldn't come back on.

For us it opened so many doors. After the concert we had our first US release

; all the record company people had come to watch.

It was one of the most important gigs of our life, which we didn't know at the time, but afterwards we went off and toured Europe with Judas Priest, who were my favourite.

It was phenomenal. It was just an honour to play there with our heroes."

Dorothy Pesch (Warlock – Vocals)

"I loved Monsters of Rock; from when I was 14-16 it was great leaving the village of Cheddar in Somerset, getting on a coach with loads of 'metallers' and it was awesome, lush, just being with a bunch of other people of a similar ilk.

The festival was wicked because it was full of people all pretty much looking the same; being part of a massive gang.

There were bottles of piss being thrown and it was really hardcore."

Jack Bessant (Reef – Bass)

"The first time I came to Donington was in 1986 when I was 12.
It was the ultimate show; Ozzy got lowered down onto the stage in a giant chair, it was amazing and fantastic, imagine being that age and seeing all that, it was incredible.
I also came in '87, '88, '90 and '91 as well."
Richie Edwards (Stone Gods – Vocals/Guitar)

"Having attended as fans over the years it was cool to have reached a stage in our career where we were invited as guests. It was a shock to realize that if you wanted to see the bands perform it was on a small TV monitor.
It was cool to hang out with so many old mates and a good place to make new contacts but if you think the Bailey's are watching Def Leppard on a piss pot TV screen, think again! We would often just piss off into the audience to watch the bands then leg it back stage.
A slice of world history was made during the 86 MOR. We ran into Def Leppard and were talking to Rick Allan and his mum who looked more nervous than he did. Rick was playing his first official gig since losing his arm in a car accident. Def Leppard made a triumphant return and when Joe Elliot turned around and said" Rick Allen on the drums" Rick got a standing ovation from the entire Donington audience. Rick's mum kindly gave the Bailey's a photo of him up on stage that day. It was also the day that we helped launch Metal Hammer magazine in the UK. We handed out thousands of flyers to the legion of

metal heads attending on the day and gave it our seal of approval.
Bad News robbed an artiste of a slot on the bill and were what you would expect, a joke.
The Scorpions were, as always, energetic, entertaining and as tight as a ducks arse. We met Ozzy Osbourne back stage and he looked scary. He had way too much black mascara on and looked out of it. Somehow he still managed to get his arse on stage and do what Ozzy does best. Mick is never shy of organizing a photo shoot so pulled Ozzy, Brian May and Phil Collen of Def Leppard together for a mug shot."
The Bailey Brothers (Mick & Dez Donington Comperes)

"I started running the site in 1986, I was the site manager. I ran it from 1986, right through to 1996."
Stuart Galbraith (ex – Donington Organiser)

"Record companies would do their best to get a part of it, out vying each other with tents backstage and "extras" (giveaways, girls in army uniform, helicopters etc)....and of course other stars would turn up just to support their friends on the bill. Brian May came to support Bad News - and got stopped at the gate. Bad News were a controversial addition to the bill – they were pretty scared beforehand, probably quite rightly too, 72,500 bone fide rock fans were a tough audience to play to."
Judy Totton (Monsters Of Rock PR)

"This was my third visit to MOR, 1985 had been good but nowhere near as good as 84, however, that was largely down to the lineup for me, I could not stand ZZTop so their lacklustre (boring to be honest) headliner performance marred my day. '86 was a different kettle of fish altogether; I loved most of the lineup so this one was always going to live up to expectations.

The weather was hit and miss all day but the atmosphere was great as usual, Donington has always retained its friendly and good humoured atmosphere and there has always been a sense of togetherness, this is not something that I have felt at most of the other festivals that I have attended.

First band on were Warlock who were fronted by the pin-up rock chick favourite of the day, Doro Pesch. The band faired well and played a crowd pleasing set without getting too many missiles chucked in their direction, these of course were saved for the next band..........Bad News.

Bad News was the fake band consisting of members of the 'Comic Strip Presents', Ade Edmonson, Rick Mayall, Peter Richardson and Nigel Planer. They came on to a rapturous bottling which did not let up until they left about half hour later. I don't think that the crowd appreciated having the piss taken out of them, although this was a great success on TV and we all loved it, this simply did not work as well live. The band stumbled their way through about three songs and spent the rest of the time getting us to shout 'Fuck Off' and other profanities at them, this was later edited and formed part of the More Bad News. I for one was not that bothered by them and *found it quite amusing that some people in the crowd were getting so worked up, however, I could not wait for some real music to begin again.*

Motorhead were next on and got the crowd going quickly with heavy as fuck tracks like opener 'Iron Fist' newish track 'Killed by Death' and of course 'Ace of Spades'. All was going well until some dick threw a lit flare on to the stage! Lemmy quickly stopped the set and went mental, threatening to kick the shit out of the culprit if they dared to come on stage and face up to their wrongdoing. This interruption fortunately did not last long or spoil my enjoyment of the set. As they neared the end of their set a Bomber flew over the crowd, this obviously was not a coincidence and had been planned to great effect, I was impressed anyway.

During the interval I saw this bloke walking towards us carrying a vast tray of beers, so many in fact that he was having trouble getting his arms around them, he got to within two metres of us when a huge missile (which I think was a half full five litre cordial type container) came out of the sky and hit his tray. He lost the lot and went crazy, he started to rant and rave about the bastard bottler taking his soul or something along those lines, he then burst into tears and fell to the ground and started to pound the chip and urine covered grass with his fists, this was the one and only time I have witnessed anyone crying at Donington (but not the last time that I would witness a tray of drinks getting knocked out of someone's grasp.

Despite the rain that that had just started, I was really looking forward to the next band, Def Leppard, I was a huge fan of 'Pyromania' which I had played to death for at least a year, this was my first change to see them after their lengthy hiatus caused by the never ending recording of 'Hysteria' and also because of Rick Allen's terrible car accident. I was not disappointed, a huge crowd of us sang and bounced along to every track, we particularly went mental during 'Photograph'. During this track our colleague Teapot decided to try his hand at crowd surfing; we were about half way back and just stood and gazed in amazement as he was thrown into the air getting nearer and nearer the front until he disappeared into the security pit at the front of stage. We did not see him again until the very end of the gig.

Def Leppard came and conquered, and I did not think it could get any better until that is the Scorpions hit the stage. At that point in time Scorpions were another of my favourite bands and I expected them to put in a tight performance, but Christ, they were absolutely fantastic.

They stormed the stage with so much energy and enthusiasm it was impossible not to get won over, highlights for me were 'Blackout', 'Big City Nights', 'The Zoo', 'Bad Boys Running Wild' and closing track 'Cant Get Enough' which of course included their patented human pyramid routine. That was easily one of the best and tightest sets I have ever witnessed at any festival and makes me smile just thinking about it - Rudy and the boys done good.

After Scorps we finally found the other half of our group that had wondered off for a piss three hour ago and of course spent a few minutes reminiscing about *the Scorps and Leps sets. One of the biggest problems with festivals in those days was finding people when they got lost, no matter how hard you tried to use a flag or the legendary pizza bus as a point of reference, it was virtually impossible finding people in the mass of denim and leather, we all looked so similar. This of course is not a problem nowadays, the invention of the mobile phone has ensured that no matter where you get lost or how stupid you are, and you can always find your friends again (unless they don't want to be found).*

Another staple at Donington (and other fests) is the dusk tradition of the good old bonfire! In good weather many people turn up in just a T-Shirt forgetting the fact that by sundown they will start to feel the chill no matter how much alcohol they have consumed. This of course requires action and this is when people's minds turn to nice toasty camp fires. They say that there are three elements to fire: fuel, oxygen and ignition, all of these are readily available at any outdoor show. Oxygen is obviously everywhere, fuel has been thrown about all day and is readily available in bottle or cardboard form covering every inch of ground and last but not least we have ignition, which is in abundance via lighters which of course have been used throughout the day to light cigarettes and other slightly less legal variants and will also be used later to hold aloft during a headliner ballad."

Roger Moore (Glinton, Peterborough)

"It was 1986 and off me and my friends went to Donington after going to the M.O.R .party at the

Derby Rockhouse the night before with the Bailey Bros as the house dj's I was a little worse for wear, but being cheered up by winning a Phonogram promo cap I was looking forward to the day ahead.
Having watched Warlock, Bad News and the return of the mighty Leps, I decided to go and meet up with my friends Nick and rich.
They came down waving two backstage passes I could not believe it, just been backstage but there's not really any one there they said, how did you get them I asked. Seen these lads with 2 passes and we said give us your passes mate and true enough they did.
I was gob smacked Rich said if you want them you and Ribs go in while we watch Motorhead so off we went in; could not believe it backstage at Donington! I was like a kid in a sweet shop in we walked not many people about so we decided to sample the backstage beer, after one or two I was rubbing my eyes and in strolls Doro and Niko from Warlock, I thought I'd had one to many.
So I made haste and got her to sign my tour book, awesome, had a chat with them and they made there way to the bar , then I turned round and I could not believe my eyes return of the thunder god Mr Rick Allen after wetting myself I calmed myself down and made an approach ,
'Rick can you sign my program' I said and give him the book
He said 'you will have to hold it for me', I felt about two inches tall ,giving a one armed man a program and a pen at the same time how does he hold it ..

He saw the funny side and signed my book and we had a good chat. I then returned to watch Scorpions and told the lads of my experience not to say I had the piss taken out of me all night,
But what the hell I had an amazing day long live the Leps....."
Jamie Taylor (Belper, Derbyshire)

"In comparison, 1986 was overcast and very cold. This contributed to the fact that our gang was depleted this year, with only half a dozen or so attending.
Ozzy put on a great show, being lowered to the stage on a giant throne. Even though the weather wasn't great, the sound was very good. I think he was introduced on stage by Tommy Vance (but it could have been Jonathon King).
Once again I decided to venture to the front of the stage, this time to watch Scorpions who very rarely disappoint. I was rewarded by capturing one of Hermann Rarebell's (used) drumsticks at the end of the set. This is still in my possession.
The highlight of Motorhead's set was the fly over by a bomber aircraft. The low point being Lemmy's bad mood and predicting (wrongly) how Motorhead would headline the following year's festival.
Def Leppard's set was predictably emotional, as it was the return of Rick Allen following his car crash. But alas they have never been my cup of tea, so beyond the curiosity factor I didn't pay them too much attention.
Why was Bad News (a TV spoof band) put on the bill above Warlock (a bona fide rock group)? Fair

enough, Warlock weren't the greatest band in the world but they had their moments and of course……they had Doro. Probably the best photo in any of the Donington programmes was the one of Doro in leather trousers with a red crotch.
A day of mixed performances, fortunately Ozzy was on tiptop form."
Paul Hartshorn (Chesterfield)

1987
Bon Jovi
Dio, Metallica, Anthrax, WASP, Cinderella, The Bailey Brothers

Monsters Of Rock '87 was unlike any other year; all of the line-up was made up of bands from the USA.
Glam metal and thrash were the flavours of the day with classic sets from most bands concerned.

Opening band, in the torrential rain, was Cinderella from Philadelphia. Already popular thanks to the constant video play for the single 'Shake Me' and the fact that their album 'Night Songs' was released almost a year to the day before they played at the festival and so was well known amongst the rock fraternity.

W.A.S.P. were also making their debut, but they would return in five years, but nothing would compare to their 'shock rock' show in 1987. With a large wooden wardrobe on stage as the main prop and a topless woman inside as the other prop, Blackie Lawless of W.A.S.P. proceeded to torture her and cut her throat with a large machete; Alice Cooper style theatrics gone mad!!!

The music was excellent, culling tracks from the 'W.A.S.P.' and 'The Last Command' albums, plus the anthem 'Animal (Fuck Like A Beast), which had made them so popular, in a bad way, with the PMRC led by Tipper Gore in the States.

Next was a double dose of thrash; Anthrax making their first appearance and Metallica making their all conquering return.

Anthrax's Joey Belladonna sang 'Indians' in full Native American headdress and the rest of the band wandered the stage, looking like a gathering of 'surf bums' in their Hawaiian shorts and t-shirts.

Metallica played their first Donington with Jason Newsted now on Bass as the replacement for the sadly departed Cliff Burton. Five tracks were played from 'Master Of Puppets', three tracks from 'Ride The Lightning', two tracks from 'Kill 'Em All' and a few covers. Metallica played mid afternoon, but it would still be another 19 years before they would come back to Donington to play all of 'Master Of Puppets' track by track, including the very rarely played 'Orion' for the anniversary tour of the albums release.

Dio was back after a four year gap, having now scaled the bill to the special guest slot. With a band that now featured the astonishing guitar skills of Craig Goldy (who is still in the band today), the audience was treated to the best of Black Sabbath ('Heaven And Hell' and 'Neon Knights'), Rainbow ('Man On A Silver Mountain' and 'Long Live Rock 'N' Roll') and the best of Dio (including 'Holy Diver', 'Stand Up And Shout', 'Last In Line' and 'Rainbow In The Dark'); an awesome appetizer for the Bon Jovi headline slot.

Bon Jovi at the time in '87 were riding high on the success of the 'Slippery When Wet' album and Donington at the time was probably one of their biggest shows; eight of the ten tracks on the album were played on the day, with a selection from the previous two albums.

For the final encore of 'We're An American Band' by Grand Funk Railroad, Bon Jovi were joined onstage by Paul Stanley (Kiss), Dee Snider (Twisted Sister) and Bruce Dickinson (Iron Maiden); Bruce let the 'cat out of the bag' that he would be back to headline with Iron Maiden the following year and Kiss would make their debut the following year as well.

Jon Bon Jovi was wearing a beard at Donington for this performance and looked very unlike his usual clean cut, boy next door, rock star image.
This year was also the first appearance for the Bailey Brothers, the music channel Rock & Metal poster boys and they recorded a lot of interviews and footage backstage for MTV; they would also return to host the show in 1988.

"It was our first Donington with Jason; we had played the '100 Club' a couple days before as a little 'warm up' gig. I believe we had our first backdrop, 'Crash Course In Brain Surgery', a Pushead take on the Budgie song.
I remember there was a lot of expectation that day; I remember the general reception in the British media was that we were 'luke warm' that afternoon; I'm not sure that I remember us being radically different in our performance of luke warm?
I remember Jason having these baggy camouflage pants, on that may have been the most visual thing onstage, other than the Pushead backdrop.
It was a great week in London where we had played a brilliant gig at the legendary 100 Club a couple of days earlier, where the temperature far exceeded 100 degrees; probably the hottest gig we'd ever played. I remember Steve Harris from Iron Maiden was there watching us and we were like 'oh my god, Steve Harris is watching us', so I think that made us want to play better, but actually made us probably not play as good as we were nervous."
Lars Ulrich (Metallica – Drums)

"I remember that Jon came over and said that we were all going to go up on stage and sing during there show as a finale. Paul Stanley was there and some people from other bands, so I said that I'd think about it, but I didn't do it, it just wasn't me. I certainly hope that Jon doesn't hold that against me for all those years, but it was my decision and I didn't do it.
The Donington festivals were always handled so well, Maurice Jones who did all those was a really good friend, so it was nice be around people that I had known and liked for a long time.
I just remember the show being somewhat like the show that we did in 1983. It's a spectacular audience that are really into everything and they've always been extremely nice to me, as a matter of fact.
I found that both were great days, but the first one was the best, because it was the first; it was a great time and I remember them both very positively.
I'd love to play it again, with either band, Dio or Heaven And Hell."
Ronnie James Dio (Dio – Vocals)

"I remember meeting Gene Simmons and Paul Stanley that day. They were sitting in with Bon Jovi later in their set that night. Both Gene and Paul were very nice to me that day! I especially remember Ritchie Sambora coming over to me just before we went on and said..."Go out there and kick some ass ...for me" I thought that was very cool of him to do that! Then just after that Ronnie came over to my side seconds before we went on and said..."Don't be so nervous...just remember who you are!!"

That was a time in my life where there was a string of firsts....and that was one of them. Playing in front of over 80,000 people! And I knew that during my guitar solo I was going to motion to the crowd to answer me back. I would play a short memorable guitar melody and then motion to the crowd to sing it back to me! Well needless to say I was very nervous about that, but after a couple of times they all were glad to oblige me and 80,000 voices answered my guitar! That was a day to remember.....I know...I should know the year...but the plaque is in a storage unit in Colorado and I'm currently trying to get it back...it used to remember the date for me as it was a proud thing to display on my studio wall and will again!!"
Craig Goldy (Dio – Guitar)

"Playing Donington 1987 was the biggest show we have ever played crowd wise up until that point in our career.
I remember arriving for soundcheck and watching DIO come out on stage to do his soundcheck; it was my first time seeing Dio perform live and meeting him. We then went on stage after Dio to perform our soundcheck. We all left after soundcheck and then returned to the venue the next morning.
It was raining as it always is in England.
The line up if I recall correctly was Cinderella, Wasp, Anthrax, Metallica, Dio and Bon Jovi.
I was able to catch a few songs from everyone that day and enjoyed all the performances that I saw.
That day was my first time meeting Steve Harris from Iron Maiden as well. Steve was nice enough to invite

me, Danny Spitz, Frank Bello and Chris Holmes back to his house that night after the show. We spent the evening there eating Indian food, playing pool and just having fun. Our show was great; it was total mayhem from start to finish.

It was a great experience and the fans did not let us down."

Joey Belladonna (Anthrax – Vocals)

"Lets put it this way, There are some guys in this world that like to go out and Rock'N' Roll and kick some ass, there are some other guys that want to stay home and wash dishes and wear aprons and I Ain't one of those"

Blackie Lawless (W.A.S.P. – Vocals/Bass)

"1987 was an amazing year for the Bailey Brothers, to be on the MOR bill with some of the world's major stars like Bon Jovi and Metallica is something we are very proud of. We were the only British act on the American dominated bill. We wanted to bring something different to the MOR in terms of a visual and audio show. Our idea was to have a huge screen that the audience could watch our videos on. We also wanted a camera filming us back stage interviewing the performers and guests thus bringing the whole event to the fans.

Unfortunately, those facilities were not provided as requested but we still managed to entertain the fans with a mix of good music and the Bailey's banter.

 MOR 1987 highlighted the great divide between Glam and Metal and you had the 80's hairspray brigade getting bottles of piss thrown at them from *the Metal fans. Somebody had to get out their and pull the fans together before trouble erupted and we rose to the challenge. The response through out the day from the fans was tremendous; to see and hear 70.000 fans singing along with you and clapping their hands is just a real adrenalin rush. Everyone always reports on the bands but with out the fans there is no show and we thank all of them for making us so welcome at the Monsters Of Rock. We also thank Maurice Jones and his team for the opportunity.*

Rock Not POP!

During the day we encouraged the fans to write in to BBC Radio One and demand more rock on the radio. We called this petition Rock Not Pop and our catch phrase was born. In the weeks that followed the station was inundated with letters which resulted in them playing rock in the day time. It was good whilst it lasted but at least we made our point.

Back stage the highlight for us was being with Paul Stanley and Gene Simmons of Kiss. It would turn out to be one of many close encounters with the legends."

The Bailey Brothers (Mick & Dez Donington Comperes)

"My first time at the festival was in 1987 when I came over with Anthrax. I was working with them at the time and it was not only my first time at Donington but my first time in England.

I recall the guys in Anthrax "bombing" my room the first night, shaving cream in the bed, etc. Made it very difficult to sleep that first night!

I recall the size of the mosh pit that day and that Scott Ian made me shoot the entire performance from the side of the stage. This is when video cameras where the size of a brick! Not fun but still an incredible thing to see."
Eddie Trunk (USA Rock Radio DJ)

"I did a second Donington in 1987, the infamous "all-American" festival. The headliner was Bon Jovi. I was there with Anthrax. Metallica played also. The sound companies were Rocksound (from Germany) and Malcolm Hill. Hill had a huge (and very good sounding) system flanking the main Rocksound speakers. I remember reading a telling article in Kerrang! the day before the show. The essence of the piece was an extremely perceptive whinge about the Donington show sound. The author had attended many a show there and wondered why, given the virtual mountain of speakers, all the opening acts sounded weak and puny whilst the headliner sounded massive. What if you didn't give a toss about the headliner? Your favorite(s) sounded lame! Shouldn't every band sound good? You paid your hard earned pounds to see and hear all the bands. The author had heard this at all the Donington Park shows and was quite fed-up. Though I feel the situation in 1981 was certainly not deliberate sabotage on the part of either AC/DC or the Malcolm Hill company, the show in 1986 was quite another story. As usual, we arrived the day before and did a good sound check. The same system engineer was there from Malcolm Hill, we reminisced about the '81 show and I remarked how

good the current iteration of the Hill system sounded. The vibe was pleasant, everything sounded fine. The next day, of course, everything was different. I had high hopes for a fine show, but as we began I noticed that the system sounded much quieter than the day before and the dynamics were limited. Nothing sounded quite right. At one point I became quite disgusted and took a little walk to my left, the centre of the mixing platform, and took a look at the system drive racks. Yes, there it was, a DBX 165 Stereo Limiter, and, by golly, it was kicking back about 12db on every peak. And it was attached to my mix! I turned to the Rocksound system tech (the sound man for the Scorpions, by the way) and asked, "What the hell is this?" I got a reply burned into my brain even these many years later: "You know how it is!" (Imagine a German-tinged accent and a condescending smile.)

Just in case you are thinking, Ahh, the Malcolm Hill people were engineering a payback for '81; not at all. Malcolm's system tech was quite embarrassed and upset. Remember, his system is attached to the Rocksound array. If it sounds like ass, his system will sound like ass. And ass it was, through every act until Bon Jovi. Then it was all it could be ("You know how it is!").

After Metallica's less than audible set, Peter Mensch (Metallica's manager with Cliff Burnstein) came up to Big Mick (Metallica's super-fine soundman) and me and he was livid. He knew that his band had been badly treated, but alas, there was nothing he could do. So it goes in the wonderful world of big-time sound. Attitudes like this limit audience enjoyment *and essentially rob the audience of what is rightfully theirs: a full and effective show. It's also a pussy move. It implies the headliner does not have the confidence to carry the show without kneecapping the competition. Does this always happen? No, but it happens often enough to be a real problem for touring professionals. It is an unfortunate part of the politics of the music business. These decisions are almost always band decisions implemented by management with the complicity of the sound company. Are there bands that make it a policy of not doing this?"*

George Geranios (Sound Engineer)

"1987 had been another good year that I enjoyed immensely, the highlights for me included a surprisingly mature and entertaining headline set from Bon Jovi which included Jon climbing to the top of the stage for one song and the crowd pleasing turn of having Dee Snider, Bruce Dickinson and Paul Stanley join him on stage for a strange but excellent version of 'We're an American Band', I considered it strange because Bruce looked ill at ease and obviously is not American, the only reason I think he was on the stage anyway was to announce that Maiden would be headlining the following year. Another memory I hazily have occurred during Metallica. Part way through the set someone managed to get past security and onto the stage where he managed to find a rope to climb and proceeded to use it as a swing, he managed to keep this up for at least a minute before being collared by

the tardy security that had let him slip through their ranks, he received a tremendous applause.

Jovi, Anthrax and Metallica's sets aside, my other favourite memory of the day was the entertainment supplied by my friend Mat who had designed his own Anthrax T Shirt with various felt tip pens in a primary school stylee, this was by far the worst shirt I have ever seen anyone wear at a gig and was ridiculed by virtually everyone that passed us, which of course had us howling with laughter all day long. Mat also learned later in the day that you should not accept drinks in medicine bottles from mad Irish men; I very much doubt he remembers Bon Jovi after a heavy dose of Pocine.

Another vague recollection I have is of Cronos from Venom stamping on my friends hand as he came stomping through the crowd trying to look all rock star cool, oh how we chuckled.

Female attendance appeared to be a lot higher this year than during the previous fests, this probably had something to do with Bon Jovi playing but it was good to see that more girls/women were enjoying what had/has largely been a male dominated and attended genre. The numbers did not seem to dissipate during the following years and continues to this day at Download. An amusing anecdote I always remember, referring to the early eighties was of how strange it always seemed, that David Coverdale would always be thrusting his crotch suggestively at the crowd at his gigs when the attendees largely consisted of teen or early 20's males.

WASP were probably the only band that disappointed me in '87, they were ok but I was expecting better. It had not been that long ago when WASP were considered the most dangerous, noisy, parent scaring band on the planet, they were raw, unpredictable and even a little bit scary, they even managed to get their first single 'Animal, Fuck Like a Beast' banned which of course made them even more desirable to fans. This of course was before the likes of Metallica and their other thrash comrades who now made WASP sound wimpy and possibly a little bit silly. Blackie Lawless and the boys did their best and they rattled through their set professionally enough churning out favourites which included 'I wanna Be Somebody' and 'Blind In Texas' but for me the feeling of danger that got me into them had vanished and I was no longer finding them enjoyable. On the day though and despite the rain during their set, they went down well enough."

Roger Moore (Glinton, Peterborough)

"I had been to concerts before, but never a festival, so I didn't know what to expect.
It was 6.30ish and I am at my local train station waiting for friends to meet up for the trek to Liverpool to catch the coach to the Monsters Of Rock , I had my leather jacket on and my metal patch denim over the top bleached knotted dyed jeans and my Air Wair boots, the real look of metal.
I noticed one of my friends Lee was there before me. He was lying on a bench with his stomach contents lying on the floor next to him; he had been there all night after his girlfriend had thrown him out because he was drunk.
It wasn't long before everyone of us had met up and

were waiting to get on the coach to the festival , Liverpool was swarming with metal heads a vast see of leathers and chanting of 'Donington Donington Donington' , excitement grew and loads of beer got drunk on the way down, before we got on the driver said no drink allowed on the coach, as soon as I sat down I was handing out swigs out of my bottles of Mad Dog 20/20 and cans of ale, everyone got their drinks onboard, the coach had a video player on it and someone had made a VHS tape of the bands playing that day and we sang along all the way, backsides shown as 'bum salutes' to fellow festival travellers and food fights between the back half of the coach and the front broke out . We started to slow down and traffic jams started, looking out the window every vehicle had people going to the festival in them. I knew we were nearly there, cars were parked up on both sides of the road and hordes of rockers making the final part on foot. "Welcome to Castle Donington Monsters Of Rock '87 the signed said, we were there. Being young at the time I drank as much as I could and staggered off down to the front to stay there and fight for my place to see the rock gods, nowadays it's: watch a band, go the bar, watch a band, go the bar and so on, I could turn around in the sea of people head banging in unison to the tunes, the Dunlop bridge hovering over the crowd in the background. We moved back towards the sound stage tower just to get breath before Bon Jovi came on stage. I will never forget we got standing behind two very drunk guys that were finding it hard to stand straight; they had plastic bottles of Scrumpy Jack everywhere around them and were chugging away on them. One of them picked one up and started to pee in one as they had no way of getting out the crowd; putting it back at his feet after he finished, the other guy, his friend, ten minutes later picked it up turned around and started talking to my friend, he then offered my mate a drink he said 'no thanks' with a grin on his face, the guy turned around and started drinking it, the people in the crowd around us just fell apart laughing.

Dee Snider, Bruce Dickinson and Paul Stanley came on stage with Bon Jovi and did a cover of 'Travelling Band' that rounded off a superb day at Donington, and I couldn't wait for the following year."

Paul Townsend (Widnes)

"My friend Tina was a massive Bon Jovi fan totally besotted by Jon.
She hung around the gate to the backstage area, where if you looked through you could see limos coming in to drop off the bands.
She saw Bon Jovi's car arrive and pushed passed the security guy, through the gate, ran towards the car and threw herself on top of the bonnet!
The car came to a quick halt, the back door opened and Dee Snider got out, he said "Hey, what's going on, god I've got crazy fans!" he looked very pleased to see Tina on all fours, quite a sight in her leopard

print mini skirt, bra top, boots and blond big hair... Then Tina jumped down off the car, ran up to him, pointing in his face and said indignantly "Who the hell are you? You're not Jon Bonjovi, what the hell are you doing here?!!" He looked a bit deflated but not as pissed off as Tina!"
Naomi Laughton (Rotherham, South Yorkshire)

"The triumphant return of Bon Jovi. Whether they were your cup or tea or not, at the time they put on a fantastic show (including lasers.......was this the first time lasers had been used at Donington?). Our gang had tripled in number from the previous year, bolstered by several females which seemed to be reflected in the overall attendance. Donington had become sexy.
I remember Jon Bon Jovi performing part of the set from the top of the lighting rig.
As part of the encore, the band was joined on stage by Dee Snider (Twisted Sister), Paul Stanley (KISS) and Bruce Dickinson (Iron Maiden). At the end Bruce saluted the crowd with a "see ya next year", which indicated that Iron Maiden were in line to play the following years Donington.
The fireworks display at the end of the show was as impressive as ever.
Dio put on their usual highly professional, faultless performance, but somehow they just didn't seem to fit in 1987.
Metallica and Anthrax passed me by I'm afraid.

WASP were a little more theatrical and Blackie Lawless' voice came over very powerful.
Bon Jovi stable mates Cinderella had an impressive debut album out at the time and their performance justified their addition to the bill. 'Night Songs' and 'Nobody's Fool' being particularly strong songs.
The weather was 'on and off' wet."
Paul Hartshorn (Chesterfield)

1988
Iron Maiden

KISS,
David Lee Roth,
Megadeth,
Guns n' Roses,
Helloween,
The Bailey Brothers

Probably remembered mostly for being the saddest year in the history of the festival, due to the heartbreaking death of two young music fans. Due to bad weather the previous few days, parts of the site had transcended into a mud bath; nowhere was it worse than in front of the stage. With everyone jumping up and down, moshing and crowd surges, the quality of the ground underfoot grew worse during the first band Helloween and the build up to Guns N' Roses.

Helloween from Germany went down well, but the most anticipated band of the day were Guns N' Roses making their MOR debut.

When GNR were originally booked they were nowhere near the popularity level that had reached by the time the festival had come around in August. With the release of the 'Appetite For Destruction' album GNR were catapulted to almost instant stardom. Slash was the guitarist that everyone wanted to emulate and Axl was the singer that everyone wanted to be.

The crowd grew as the GNR set loomed closer and as the band started up it could be seen that there was a problem; jostling fans caused massive crowd surges and the slippery ground underfoot meant that sections of the crowd were falling over and then people from behind them were piling on top of them, some people had no chance of getting out. Give the band their due, Axl did stop the concert several times and ask the people further from the stage to move a few steps back, in order to allow the people at the front space to breathe and help people up that had fallen in the crush. At the time the extent of the chaos wasn't known to most of the people in attendance and the security staff were fighting a losing battle, unable to get into the crowd during the bands performance.

All the sad news would be all over the BBC news that night and the following day; a dark cloud had descended over Donington and would be remembered by all in attendance whenever Donington 1988 was mentioned.

Up next were Megadeth, with Mustaine in fine mood for a set in the mid afternoon; this was their debut at Donington and 2010 will be their hat trick of festival appearances.

Next up was David Lee Roth making his return to Donington after 4 years; this time his guitar maestro was Steve Vai in the position that was filled by Eddie Van Halen in Van Halen. Steve Vai was an ex- Frank Zappa guitar prodigy who had played on the album 'Ship Arriving Too Late To Save A Drowning Witch'; Vai would return to Donington as lead guitarist in Whitesnake, in the headliner position, two years later in 1990.

Special guest this year was none other than the 'mighty' Kiss, without make-up, making their first of three appearances to date.

Playing a mixture of classic and recent songs, Kiss could do nothing but entertain the masses. The line-up featured Bruce Kulick and Eric Carr; the die hard fans were still yearning for a 'full make-up Kiss' playing all the classic 'Alive; tracks, 7 years later at Donington they would get their wish.

Headliner Iron Maiden made their first appearance at Donington and what a performance it was. Another British band topping the bill and a band that could fill the slot with ease.

Playing tracks from most of their albums, including crowd pleasers 'Run To The Hills', 'Number Of The Beast', 'The Trooper' and 'Aces High'.

So another festival drew to a triumphant close, only tarnished by the two fan deaths during the GNR set; the names of Alan Dick and Landon Siggers would be forever etched on the Donington history for all the wrong reasons.

Due to the tragic events in 1988 the festival took a sabbatical in 1989, returning two years later, with increased security, precautionary measures and a greatly reduced capacity.

"You can't argue with a crowd this big and we don't intend to argue, we intend to entertain"
Paul Stanley (Kiss – Vocals/Guitar)

"I was amazed at the enormous crowd and the very metal attitude that was at the Festival.

Gene and Paul were excited even though Iron Maiden headlined. We had such a good hit with 'Crazy Nights'; the fans were very into the band. The stage was SO huge, and that was really cool to be on it. Paul loved the ramps which he used, and what a feeling to look out at the crowd and see so many people out there, like an ocean of fans! The pressure was on, but we played great and I remember us all being pleased.

I watched some of G n' R and I was impressed with the reaction. Sad of course that some fans died getting crushed to see them. Backstage, there was press, lots of cool people and quite a good hang for everyone. I still meet people in the industry who say they met me backstage at Donington!

We left while Iron Maiden was doing their thing, and I remember leaving the grounds knowing it was an event that will be remembered for many fans for a long time. I still have the tour book and the souvenir mug!"

Bruce Kulick (Kiss – Lead Guitar)

"If every one of these guys had bought the album we would be doing great.   I came here thinking this would be the worst day of my life after hearing all the horror stories about Donington but it's the best day of my life".

We are not going to be one of these bands that make an album then disappear"

Axl Rose (Guns N' Roses – Vocals)

"The good and the bad goes on here. I found out the responsibility of a band being huge right here. When Guns played here, the first time the band had got really big in the UK and between getting booked on the bill and the time we played the band had blown up, so we were lower down on the bill; everybody surged forward when we played and that was before they had the partitions and two guys drowned in the mud.

So this festival for me also has a really serious aspect to it. This is where I grew up and realised, 'Oh shit. Nobody told me about all this.' This kind of stuff, the responsibility. You start thinking that if the band never got big then those two guys would still be alive; you go through that stuff in your head."
Duff McKagan (Guns N' Roses – Bass)

"The last time I played here in 1984 Van Halen was peaking, as do all great relationships but the audience were spectacular.
The whole theory of Rock 'N'Roll in England and Europe is different to America."
David Lee Roth (David Lee Roth – Vocals)

"My memory of the gig was that it was massive in terms of size. I'd heard of the Donington event and expected it to be a large crowd but was still blown away by the shear size of the whole thing.
I remember that we played Donington during a period in which Dave was trying to change his image to be "classier" so he had us all wearing suits. At that time Dave wanted to distance himself form the other bands that wore leather and blue jeans or the loud spandex clothes from which he had become associated with just a couple of years earlier. Things were also coming to a head with his relationship with Steve Vai and the "gunslinger" mentality for which he was hired in the first place. I think it was also around that time Vai had gotten a big money offer from David Coverdale to join Whitesnake, which also made things tense out there.

Before the gig Dave and the band discussed the set list, which included songs like 'California Girls', 'Just A Gigolo' and 'Just Like Paradise' that were more in a pop vain. Some of the band thought we should leave out those songs and do a set that featured the harder material rather than the commercial songs because it was of course Donington. Kiss was headlining that day and there were a lot of harder bands like Guns n' Roses and others on the bill.
Well, we did our regular set without change and the crowd responded great and we left with a sense that we had left an impression on the audience regardless of the suits or the set list selection. But there was no question that the Vai era was coming to a close and I was bummed to see that happening.
I also remember being pretty impressed with Paul Stanley's voice. Donington was the first time I'd ever heard Kiss live. They really did rock and the crowd loved them. I've always respected their impact on music and especially their contribution to the theatrical part of rock and roll. Hats off to them…."
Brett Tuggle (David Lee Roth – Keyboards)

"I have played bigger in my dreams."
Dave Mustaine (Megadeth – Vocals/Guitar)

"Donington 1988 was the first big festival I had played and it had a significant place in my world because I used to listen to the Castle Donington album when I was about 17 years old. That record featured Rainbow (with Graham Bonnet), April Wine, Scorpions and a bunch of other cool up and coming bands of that time. This was when I was at home in

Minnesota, before I moved to California and met Dave Mustaine. I remember going 'wow this is friggin' great' because I was getting into all those bands at that time.

I played in '88 on the 'So Far, So Good, So What?' album and Maiden headlined; they were on their 'Seventh Son Of A Seventh Son' album and we played 7 dates with them on that tour, in America just before.

So Castle Donington just sounded awesome, coming from America there was always this affinity and infatuation with Europe and all bands starting out wanted to get to Europe.

So coming over here was huge and to play Castle Donington was the moment that 'you had arrived'.

Donington is an event for everyone and everyone who's anyone is always there, either as a performer or spectator. The day I played there I recall pulling up in the tour bus and there were 107,000 people in attendance. Literally farther than the eye could see.

You can always tell Download because of the barricade split down the middle. So, every time you see a photo you know that it was Download or even AC/DC live at Donington, because you can see that gap and it's a tell tale sign of any 'live' photo.

I remember flying in and meeting the Guns N' Roses guys at the airport. I think that they had been touring America with Aerosmith and they flew the Concorde over, bastards!

So the part of the video footage in the 'Paradise City' music video, where you see the Concorde, that's them, flying to Donington.

So we met at a truck stop and got something to eat with Steven Adler along the way, as our bands were friends in LA.

When they played they were kicking ass, they were just great. I remember seeing them open for the Cult when they were this little 'Hollywood bar band' on these big stages. The record was taking off and I remember thinking 'wow' these guys had really spent some time on big stages.

Guns n' Roses played before us and unfortunately 2 people were killed in the audience and I think that after that they stopped having it for a while then reorganised it and eventually it became Download.

David Lee Roth was after us, with Kiss and Iron Maiden to follow. We left when Kiss were playing, so we didn't see Maiden.

The stand out memory in 1988 was that the fans would throw 2 liter bottles of urine at the stage, presumably because they were smashed in so tight in the crowd that they couldn't 'relieve' themselves from their beer consumption any other way than to pee on the ground or in the bottle they just drank from. Having no where to put it they simply threw it at the band!

They were also throwing huge clumps of mud which made for good sport while trying to thrash. In fact, using my bass guitar as a defensive shield against the trash being at the stage was as much fun as the actual show itself On a personal note, that was the kind of the last show for me. I was at the end of a very old life for me; I did a lot of drugs and I was really 'strung out'. To be honest, it was kind of bitter sweet for me because I remember showing up there

and thinking I had worked my whole life for this and it was a dream, I was standing on the stage at Donington, sick as a dog, feeling like shit and I remember that after that I went home and started the re-hab circuit."
David Ellefson (Megadeth – Bass)

"I was here for Rainbow in 1980 - I had waited all my life for this moment."
Chuck Behler (Megadeth – Drums)

"I was really excited, to see Guns n' Roses and David Lee Roth, who was brilliant, really brilliant, 'cept this big bloke in front who kept shouting 'DAVE' at Dave Lee Roth and trying to give him a cigar.
GNR were like giants, they were fantastic, they were brilliant."
Tony Wright (Terrorvision – Vocals)

"I went in 1988 as a paying customer with my girlfriend at the time and we'd got the bus down from Glasgow. We were drunk out of our minds.
There were around 107,000 people there that year and it was the year that unfortunately those two young lads lost their lives during Guns n' Roses; obviously the hype regarding G'N'R was huge and the crowd was just out of control. I remember being stuck in the crowd and we were in a situation where you couldn't even get your arms above your head.
We had just started the Almighty and we were about six or seven months into the bands career and I remember standing there thinking 'this is amazing; I want to be on the stage and I want to play there'.

Ricky Warwick (The Almighty – Vocals/Guitar)

"The 1988 MOR was one of the Bailey Brothers most memorable and successful performances in our history. Not only were we back on the MOR bill, we were writers and presenters of MTV's number one rated programme. This time the cameras would follow us back stage as we interviewed every band on the mega bill. They also filmed us on stage in front of over 100,000 thousands fans many chanting our catch phrase 'Rock Not Pop'.
 Kiss sent us a bottle of Champagne round to our dressing room which was a real nice touch.
Jonathan King thought he could do what the Bailey's did and just walk out on stage. I don't think anyone in the history of the MOR has had more shit thrown at them. He was covered from head to toe in mud and piss. He came up to us after the show asking for a copy of the film footage. We didn't oblige.
It was almost non stop for about fourteen hours at the 88 MOR for the Bailey Brothers.
We felt we deserved a drink after the festival and hung out with our manager at the time John Doukas. Ex Thin Lizzy guitarist Brian Robertson joined us and nearly got us kicked out of the hotel .We kept this old guy called Bert serving us until 5 AM in the morning but Robbo still wanted more and had a secret stash of lager bottles hidden behind a plant by the entrance door. We all went up to his room and as he was going to take a drink a slug appeared from the bottle and Brian was screaming at the top of his voice," look a Fookin' wee little beastie". He still drank from the bottle as the hotel manager came to try and remove

us. We had put the slug in the bath and told the manager we would report him to the environmental health if he didn't leave us alone and he apologized and left us to it.

When Guns N' Roses were booked to play the MOR they were a band on their way up. It was during their set that two fans died although none of us knew at the time. By the time they hit the stage they were the band everybody wanted to see. In all the years of MOR it had never been this full.

Sadly one of the greatest rock and Metal concerts in British history will always be tinged with sadness".

RIP Alan Dick and Landon Siggers"

The Bailey Brothers (Mick & Dez Bailey Donington Comperes)

"But the fans themselves were always the best, always polite and always there just for the music (with the bonus of beer and bottle throwing of course...). Apart from the tragic year the two boys died there was very little trouble, very few arrests, maybe six or seven. Donington was immensely hard work, we took it seriously but we loved it. It played a major part in my life for more than a decade and I rather enjoyed being queen of the rock chicks for a day. I even received a 'Music Week' Top PR Award for my work on it so we must have been doing something right!"

Judy Totton (Monsters Of Rock PR)

"Iron Maiden and their soundman Doug Hall, for years they challenged any band to blow them off the stage and would provide all the watts they needed to

try. As a matter of fact, the 1988 Donington featured Iron Maiden and Doug assembled a huge sound system. Doug gave everybody everything and our Big Mick attested to this. He was once again in attendance (in what capacity I don't recall). I saw him later at another festival and he gave the sound system his highest accolade: "Raging." The 100,000 plus music fans got their money's worth that day. I hope this little missive informed and enlightened those of you who are interested in these sorts of sordid details. Alas, my many years as a soundman were full of moments like these. But, like, golf, the one great shot keeps you going. The shows where the band and the sound system came together and built a powerful musical experience were some of the finest moments of my working life."
George Geranios (Sound Engineer)

"Over the next couple of years I'd started listening to heavier stuff - Faith No More had exploded onto the scene and that really expanded my musical horizons. Guns 'n' Roses were quite the buzz band and their inclusion on the bill prompted me to get a ticket. I was driving and had my own car by now, so no coach ticket was required.
One of my best mates at the time was a chap called Dave Shackleton (known to all as Shack). He's now married to Nikki Chapman (from Pop Idol) and a bigwig at Sony BMG (I haven't seen him in years) but I'd known him when he was stacking shelves at Grandways.
He was a big Rush, Saga & Sabbath fan and his ambition in the Grandways days was to be a music

journalist. In 1988 he was freelancing for Kerrang! and about to become managing editor of "Metal Forces" magazine.

Shack didn't drive and needed a ride to Donington. I had an underpowered 1.3L Capri MkIII and I gained my first guest pass to any event in exchange for a lift. I agreed, and managed to sell my ticket for just below 'face value' to a friend in Halifax.

Queuing up to get in, my fan belt went. Not a huge problem as I was there - I'd think about getting home later! Looking for the car parks, Shack said to go to the guest area. We drove up to the paddock entrance, but we didn't have a car pass! Who'd have known that your guest pass wouldn't get your vehicle in! I pulled over as the ever resourceful Shack went into the site on foot, found Malcolm Dome and borrowed his car pass for my car! Sorted. I drove my overheating car into the guest car park. I had AA Membership, but figured they wouldn't manage to get in so left it for the end of the day.

Walking into the little backstage village, there was the EMI pavilion and smaller marquees owned by the likes of Warners & Kerrang!. Girlschool were sat outside the Kerrang! tent, Vixen & Maiden were lounging around in the EMI one. Everyone had free food & drink so I was rather annoyed with my chauffeur role for the day. Kerrang! were just about to launch their 100th issue (they were bi-weekly at the time) and I had the first piece of their guitar shaped cake. At one point queuing up for the toilet Slash stumbled over me, bottle of Jack in hand.

It was a pleasant walk from there to the arena, along a line of trees behind the stage which seem to be long gone. There were people all around the entrance, offering to buy my pass off me but I ignored them and went on in. My attempts to find somewhere to get a Guns n' Roses shirt were in vain - sold out, so I had to make do with a Dave Lee Roth one. We were late in and had missed the openers Helloween, so had to watch Guns n' Roses from the top of the hill. A good job really, considering the events that it later transpired had happened - the crush during G n'R's set. We weren't really aware that anything had happened at the time, we were so far back.

Megadeth were ok, never really been my thing. Dave Lee Roth entertained as expected. Kiss were without makeup, and I found them quite dull and we returned to the backstage area to watch on the big screen in the EMI tent while Shack interviewed Vixen on the next table. Of course when Iron Maiden came on, everybody was booted out of the guest area to go and watch from the arena. It was the first time I'd seen Maiden, and they put on a great show. The latest album was 'Seventh Son Of A Seventh Son' and they had a huge set and backdrop. I think this was also the only time Kiss ever broke their promise that they would never play support to anyone who had supported them in the past...

Trudging back to the car, I remembered the fan belt. This was, of course, before mobile phones so I drove out of the gates, and there was a phone box near the Park Farm Hotel that I called the AA from. Due to the traffic it was three hours before he reached me. One new fan belt later and we were on our way home - I remember dropping Shack off just as it was getting light."

Phil Hull (Download Forum Administrator)

"1988 was the one and only time of my visiting the 'Monsters of Rock' at Donington, but it was a real eye opener.
It was the first time I'd gone to any festival, so it was a great start. Having arrived by coach early, there was a time of hanging around and waiting in anticipation. When it was time to go in, I was scared and excited all at the same time. All the hoards of people heading towards the stage area waiting for the first band – being Helloween. I was quite new to their music, but I do remember 'Dr Stein' being played and thoroughly enjoyed it. There were a couple of people in front of me throwing oranges at the stage and I was really annoyed, but I was too young and too nervous to say anything.
Guns n' Roses were fantastic. I had been looking forward to seeing them and it was just before they became well known. It was a time I still had enough room to dance to their tracks on the dance floor at the local rock night, but you just knew they were going to be really big. I would say it was the best time to see them live, Axl Rose looked stunning and you were actually able to get close enough to see. They played a really good set that included 'Mr Brownstone' and 'Paradise City' to name just two.
Megadeth were disappointing to me, but only because of all the swearing. I remember the comment of 'thanks for giving us all your f**king money'. I can remember the music being good though, but only if you could get past all the obscenities in-between.

Dave Lee Roth. What a performer! He put on a fabulous stage show and although I would have classed him as being fairly commercial, you couldn't help but enjoy yourself. He was already a legend at that time, and so it was a real treat to see him live on stage.

Kiss were on next, but this was the one band that didn't appeal so much to me personally, and so I took the opportunity to go and buy a t-shirt. It was a good idea at the time, but the only t-shirts that were left had several different bands listed on the back that didn't actually play! I remember Anthrax being listed at the bottom, and felt really gutted that they weren't actually there.

At that time, Iron Maiden was my favourite band. I worked my way up to the front and got hit on the head with a couple of two litre bottles, but did not want to think about what they contained. I was determined to stand my ground, as I'd seen them live before and had a huge crush on Bruce Dickinson. I also wanted to get a good look at Eddie on stage. If I remember correctly, it was the time of their 'Somewhere On Tour' and I had my 'Somewhere In Time' watch on (which I was very proud of). I then got hit with a small lemonade bottle and had to give up and move back, as this one really hurt. I didn't miss too much though, as they had large screens on each side of the stage that I could watch. I was on a high as they performed an amazing show - again.

The down side was when we heard about the people getting crushed at the front and later found out how serious it had been.

The day was over, but the ordeal continued with trying to find my coach. I found out that the one I should have been on was in amongst all the coaches heading for Glasgow. I didn't know this, as they weren't there when we had arrived and it was now dark, so I didn't have a clue where I was. I did manage to get on another coach heading in the same direction, but I was absolutely exhausted. My friends supposedly kept asking me questions that I had been answering in my sleep, but with answers that didn't make sense. I then woke up thinking that we'd stopped at a service station, but to find out that we had actually broken down. Looking back now though, it did add to the fond memory of a brilliant day that happened all those years ago.
Thanks for the experience Donington!"
Diane Newman (Plymouth)

"We were there with an army this time.
This year it seemed different; more excitement, much bigger, more build up than the year before and the line up was fantastic. I can honestly say it was my all time favourite line up. Helloween, Guns N' Roses, Megadeth, Dave Lee Roth (with the legend Steve Vai on guitar) Kiss and Iron Maiden. The weather was bad but that didn't put anyone off, I recall one of the video screen collapsing in the wind. The crowd was this huge, massive, energy charged monster that exploded when the first band Helloween came on stage. One second I was on the right hand side of the stage midway from the front and sound stage then a second later I was on the left side of the stage and my feet never touched the floor! I was

grabbing on to anyone around me and everyone else seemed to be holding onto me. Guns N' Roses were due to come on and the crowd was getting more packed. I could feel nothing but pain as I was squashed, but this was the band I wanted to see. Some girl got in a panic and me and a few guys got her over the crowd and carried down to the front. When they came on I have never seen or been in a crowd like that, or since. Another small girl was frantic to get out. There was no way she could escape, people were pushing people out of the way to pick her up off the floor, they got her up and managed to put on some dudes shoulder where she hung on for life, they were band of the day for me.

Iron Maiden later put on the best show they had ever done.

Sore wet drained we made our way home.

We never had mobile phones back then, when I got home in the early hours all the lights were on. I opened the door and my girlfriend was up and my family were there, she was upset I asked 'what is up?' She showed me a video of the news from that day, the news had a caption saying Guns N' Roses, but the footage was of Helloween then it said that two people had died, my heart sank, and she was upset because it could have been me."

Paul Townsend (Widnes)

"When entering the arena on this tragic day it was obvious to me that something was wrong, there appeared to be far more people attending than any previous year and obviously far more than the 80,000 'ish that I thought was the limit. The crowd usually *thinned out significantly at the back around the track area where the stalls were located, however, on this day it was even packed around this area. We later learned that there was something in the region of 107,000 there, many of which I believe had got in over the walls etc.*

We moved somewhat slower than usual to our preferred location stage left (which always seemed to have more room than the same area stage right) just as Helloween started up, these fun German nutters were riding on the success of their popular 'Keeper of the Seven Keys' opus and went down relatively piss bottle free.

During the end of Helloweens set the scaffolding and video screen on the left collapsed forward and ended up being held just above the crowds heads by the metal fence at the back, if the fence had not been there I think that the scaffolding would have ended up hitting a good few tightly packed punters underneath it.

I was yet to get into Guns N' Roses and so had no intention of trying to move further forward for their set, looking back I am glad that this was the case as who knows what would have happened if were was unfortunate enough to get caught in the crush that occurred during their set. Besides, this was the first time I had taken my girlfriend (later and still Wife) Sue to a festival and there was no way I was going to jeopardise her safety.

From our vantage point, the crowd looked rowdy but it was not until Axl started to talk about people being hurt, I forget his words exactly but at one point just before 'Welcome to The Jungle' he asked the crowd to step back as there were people unconscious. It became apparent that it was worse down there than it appeared to us, in fact we were oblivious to the severity of what had happened until the end and did not understand the it properly until we got home and turned on the news the next day. It was however apparent that the front was not the place to be and that people were being injured! During the interval after G n' R's set I saw a youngish bloke stumble passed us, covered in blood, with a garden cane sticking out of his neck, strangely he was laughing, I have no idea whether this was real or an elaborate make up job but it looked real enough to me. We also heard from passers by that people had been injured.

Although the atmosphere was somewhat less jovial than previous events we continued to enjoy the strong lineup and of course the contents of our 5 litre beer containers. Next up were Megadeth who were ok but seemed to suffer from a less than great sound, I was not overly impressed especially as the largest woman on the planet was blocking our view decked out in the most shockingly pink rain coat and matching umbrella that I have ever seen. Every time we tried to move this pink elephant seemed to move with us.

After what was surely the bottle fight to end all bottle fights, David Lee Roth was next up, and thankfully the Pink one had moved on to annoy other unfortunates. The master showman soon had us eating out of his hands as he ploughed through Van Halen classics such as 'Hot for Teacher' and 'Jump' along with his solo material, the best being 'Yankee Rose' always memorable because of the conversation he always had with Steve Via's Guitar (guitar responding to Dave's queries). Part way in to the set Dave seemed to be experiencing problems within the crowd and had to stop at least twice until calm was restored, at one point a security guard got on stage and was told to 'Get Off My Fucking Stage'. I was unsure when we first heard whether the deaths had occurred during GNR or DLR as the crowd seemed possibly denser during Dave's set.

During the next interval we decided to have a wonder around the stalls but soon gave up due to the sheer amount of people milling about, it was like wadding through treacle trying to get anywhere and had become a mammoth task just trying to get to the toilets. I felt particularly sorry for the ladies who had to endure massive queues, worse than on any other occasion at any festival I have attended to date.

A new phenomenon seemed to be emerging during this show, it was of course the human pyramid, I had never witnessed this before and it may have started elsewhere but there seemed to be a lot of people trying it out on that day, some where quite impressive and had reached at least five or six high. This of course was deemed mega fun for the bottle throwers who all aimed their missiles at the pyramids until they collapsed under the onslaught, this was a great way to spend the interval time for all concerned: pyramid builders, bottlers and observers, I remained in the latter category as I could not be bothered with either of these activities.

It was soon time for Kiss to hit the boards. The version of Kiss that graced us with its presence on this day was of course the 'Crazy Nights' era incarnation minus the make-up and to a certain extent, the fun. Musically I quite enjoyed them during the 80's and with Eric Carr and Bruce Kullick on board they were certainly way more technically proficient, however, live they were simply not the same beast without the gimmicks, pyros and most importantly the outfits. That said, I enjoyed their set but had that nagging feeling that they were not firing on all cylinders (this was proven correct when I later witnessed the original masked lineup, several times, including their stunning Donington headline of '96).

The year before, during Bon Jovi's set, Bruce Dickinson had announced that Maiden would be headlining the following year, so there was no surprise when this was confirmed in Kerrang! sometime after Christmas. At the time Maiden was still one of my favourite live bands and as it was their first appearance at Donington I was eagerly anticipating their set. Again, I was not disappointed, we were treated to arguably the best stage show of any MOR so far and one of the tightest set lists, Maiden reigned supreme on that day.

I have mixed emotions when thinking back to what was easily the most memorable of the Monsters Of Rock gigs, on one hand, the music was superb and company great as always, on the other hand, it was hard to come to terms with the fact that two people had arrived at the festival as we did, expecting to have the time of their lives but never returned home. On the plus side, the events of that day have forced changes in festival safety which have been implemented and improved ever since. I now feel incredibly safe standing near the front at Download or

elsewhere and thankfully have never witnessed that kind of chaos since.
RIP Allan Dick and Landon Siggers, you shall always be remembered."
Roger Moore (Glinton, Peterborough)

"What I can remember is the night before MOR (1988) me & my friend went to a local rock nightclub, left at 4:00am-ish grabbed a couple of hour's kip, and then headed off to meet up with some other of our mates; jumped in the back of their van and headed off.
It was the first really big rock festival we had been to. We couldn't quite believe that we were able to see so many bands on the same day! I'd never seen so many rockers in one place. They were everywhere...it was an incredible sight...I still remember the Dunlop tyre... (Now sadly gone) standing out...
It was very muddy as it rained heavily most of the time and at one point we ended up wearing the famous black bin bag
coats.
Later (after plenty of Cider) when Guns N' Roses were on, we were stood about a third of the way back, when the crowd surged forward, but my mum (back at home) panicked when she heard on the radio about two people getting crushed and remember it was in the days before mobiles. She had no way of contacting me, worse for her was that all the previous rock gigs I'd

been to, I had always been at the front. So she was very worried to say the least. So when I returned home safe. Her face was a picture.
Having said that, all in all (excluding the 2 unfortunate deaths of course) I can say it was a fantastic experience and has led to me continuing going to festivals and rock gig for over 30 years! And long may it continue."
Deborah Mowforth (debbywebby)

"1988, still at 6th form and a skinny 17yr old. I just about managed to scrape enough money to go to Donington.
I worked in a pub bottling up and one of the regulars was going with his mate to the festival from Newbury! (Can't remember his name) So myself and a good friend Mike (He introduced me to the 'Appetite For Destruction' album about 2 months before, so I couldn't wait to see them) scrounged a lift in a tiny mini metro to MOR.
Pink & purple swim shorts, a Reading Festival 1987 tour T-Shirt, doc martins, topped off with an old brown leather jacket that I bought from a friend for £10 and I was ready to ROCK.
We eventually made it to Castle Donington, my first of many MOR/DL concerts. I can remember walking over the race track near the famous tyre and looking down (the stage was at the bottom of the hill in a bowl) and the area was pretty full considering no one was on stage yet.
I think we quaffed a few lagers and made our way down for Helloween and positioned ourselves behind

one of the speaker/lighting rigs to the left hand side of the stage.

When GnR's hit the stage, wow, by that time we had ventured forward as close as possible, no room to move and then they kicked off with 'It's So Easy', I can remember all of a sudden being about 30 ft from where I was first stood. Jesus it was insane, trying to stay on your feet as the ground was a bog pit! The 1st song went by and by this time I had lost my friend Mike and the other 2 that we had come with! I was now squeezed in about 20-30ft from the front. Next song kicked off and yet again it was just a case of trying to stay on your feet. I remember helping people who had fallen or ended up on the floor, pulling them up and then bouncing along with them in the scrum.

At one point they stopped the set and asked people to move back as the people at the front were getting crushed, so for about 20-30 seconds we could breath a bit, then the next song started and back to the mass of bodies running from left to right, trying to stay upright.

At this point 1 guy had fallen over and I picked him up with another chap, he was semi conscious and we held him under his arms and started to make our way back as there was no way he could stand on his own. I remember shouting and yelling at people to 'get the f*** out the way', as myself and this complete stranger struggled to carry the chap out of the masses. As we struggled towards the speaker/lighting rig, which was fenced off, I thought my legs were wet.....and yes the chap I was carrying had thrown up all over my shorts and legs, um lovely.

All I remember then is that we eventually got this chap to the fenced off lighting/speaker area and not so much threw him but tried to place him in the safety of this area. I'm not sure what happened to this chap but I'd like to think that the 2 of us had helped him survive?

From there I ventured back away from the bouncing masses to the relative safety of mid viewing. I look back and think it was one of the scariest times I have ever experienced at a gig and only that I stayed on my feet stopped me from becoming a statistic.

After GnR's, I decided not to go to close to the front to watch the remaining bands. Although for DLR I did get right to the front, but that was it.

I didn't find any of my friends until I went back to the car after Iron Maiden. One hell of an experience and I was so hooked and had one of the most memorable days at a festival. So much so I went to MOR in Bochum Germany the following week, Awesome."

Russell Kennerley (Newbury)

"At long last British Heavy Metal heroes Iron Maiden finally got their shot at headlining Britain's top rock festival.

Their show was based around the 'Seventh Son' album. And with an impressive stage set and song selection they wowed the crowd with an excellent performance worthy of their position at the top of the bill.

However there was an impressive line up beneath them……

Kiss performed a no nonsense, no make up set, that would have set the crowd alight had it not been for a

very colourful Dave Lee Roth and co. strutting their stuff with typical American bombast and flair immediately before them. Steve Vai brought out his triple necked, heart shaped guitar at one point.
The Dave Lee Roth T-shirts were probably the best of the day also.
We all know what happened during Guns n' Roses performance, although we didn't at the time. The bands meteoric rise to superstardom had caught the organisers out (they were only second from bottom on the bill, which was probably right when they were originally booked). A sad day for rock music.
Both Megadeth and Helloween were OK, but nothing special.
The weather was windy and wet.
Due to repercussions following the deaths of the two fans during Guns n' Roses' set there was a year out in 1989."
Paul Hartshorn (Chesterfield)

"I have numerous experience's from Monsters of Rock, the first year I went was 1988 with my Mum and Dad (I was 14 and lucky for me they loved their rock music, they still do in fact!) and I was hooked. I was such a huge Maiden fan from the age of 7 as my Mum and Dad use to hammer "Number of the Beast"; so to see them in a scale so big was out of this world. I have not missed a MOR or Download since so that's quite a few years! Memories that stand out for me on this wondrous one day event (apart from the horrible drive home after drinking too much warm beer), were the human pyramids, I remember my first year attempting one, I ended up in

A & E the next day with 5 other people dressed in Monsters of Rock T-shirts who I had never met adorning the same type of bruises I had. They were definitely not for the faint hearted and luckily enough they have kind of gone out of fashion! I remember a load of us had piled down in a transit van with no windows and just a mattress for protection in the back, we pulled up near the Hallowed Turf next to 3 other transit vans who's doors opened and what seemed like hundreds of people rolling out the back, believe me if you ever wanted to know how many people you could fit into the back of a transit van.......it was a hell of a lot! Also, one thing that had always tickled me is how some people had a total utter need to wear their full tasselled leather jackets with patches and some even with the denim cut off jacket over the top in 90 degree heat!! Then again I guess that still happens but with the addition of New Rock Boots in Download Festival!!"

Jude Wright (Wallasey, Merseyside)

"During the Guns n' Roses set in 1988 and the resulting crush that unfortunately took 2 of our fellow fans, myself and a friend were about 10 metres from the barrier and feeling the pressure from all the people around us, so we decided to get the hell out of there..

As we turned to get away a girl was also trying to get out, but she was heavily pregnant; we advised going over the top of the crowd as the quickest and probably safest way out for her, but she wanted to walk out. So we got the girl between us, with my friend at the front and me at the back. We somehow managed to get all 3 (4 if you include the baby) out of that hell.

She thanked us for our help (as if we could say no) and that was the last we saw of her.

I often find myself wondering how the girl got on and hope that her baby was well and who knows might be attending the festival these years, as he/she will be what 22 years old now....I can only hope."

Martin Scott (Ayr)

"What an amazing festival line-up that was, Maiden, Kiss, Guns n' Roses, David Lee Roth, Megadeth etc.

By the time we entered the main arena we were pretty much hammered, early on we were sat near the beer tents at the back.

When Guns n' Roses came on I made my way to the front to get a better view, but Presh stayed further back to carry on his drinking, I made a note of where he was and was gonna join him in about 40 mins, this was mid afternoon and I'd left all my money, beer and food with him; I wasn't going to be long, as soon as Guns finished I was gonna make my way back to him to carry on drinking.

Problem was though, finding the fucker again. I could've sworn I knew where he was, but I must've walked round that field dozens of times trying to find the twat; nowhere to be seen!

What a bastard, never saw him again all day until we got on the bus to go home, I was starving hungry, dehydrated and dying of thirst. He'd had a great time, eaten my grub, drank my beer and spent my money, bastard.

He said he never moved from the spot, I still don't believe him."
Gary 'Fozzy' Forrester (Hull)

1990
Whitesnake
Aerosmith, Poison, Quireboys, Thunder

After the melancholy feelings of Monsters Of Rock in 1988 came the sense of elation at the festivals return two years later, with a bill that was a 60% British and 40% American. There was reduced festival capacity and more safety precautions in place; so problems like the year before would never happen again.

Making their first of three appearances at Donington (ending with their 'secret band' slot at Download 2009) Thunder opened the proceedings for the day and set the bar very high for other bands to try and achieve. Playing tracks from their debut album 'Backstreet Symphony',

Thunder were the quintessential British band, with their feet firmly stuck in the '90's but their roots in the classic rock sounds of the '70's.

Another British band was up next, the Quireboys, hailing from Newcastle with their brand of 'Faces' music for the modern rock fan. Managed at the time by Sharon Osbourne (before she hit mega stardom) the Quireboys were the ultimate party band; singing their way through a set peppered with tracks from their debut album 'A Bit Of What You Fancy'; we were covered in 'Roses And Rings',

woken up by '7 o'clock' and invited to a 'Sex Party', 70's party rock with a 90's slant.

Poison were loved enough at the time to play all their hits and have female fans drooling at the front, whilst their boyfriends hung back in the crowd waiting for Aerosmith to play. 'Talk Dirty To Me' was their most popular of the set, proving that their debut album was still the best Poison release to date and the one that the fans longed to hear tracks from.

Eventually, the wait was over and Aerosmith made their all singing, all swaggering, all sexual innuendo oozing Donington debut.

Playing a career spanning set from 1973's 'Dream On' right through to 'Love In An Elevator' from the 1989 album 'Pump'. Aerosmith were the band of the day and the most anticipated by the crowd, having not played in the UK for nearly a year. Aerosmith also pulled a masterstroke by bringing on Jimmy Page of Led Zeppelin for their encores,

which was an unexpected treat for all the avid rock fans.
Finally the headliner for 1990 was another British band, back for their 'rock 'n' roll hat-trick'; three appearances at Donington, two in the headline position and what a different beast Whitesnake were now!
The 90's Whitesnake was the 'MTV friendly' totally Americanised version of the classic British rock band. Thanks to the constant MTV airplay of the 'Snake videos for 'Is This Love' and 'Here I Go Again' (a re-recording of the original from the 'Saints & Sinners' album in 1982), Whitesnake were reaching a totally diverse audience. From AOR fans, to metal fans, to soft rock fans and fans of David Coverdale's wife to be (at the time) Tawny Kitaen, who featured heavily in the erotic styled videos, the 'Snake was slithering its way across America and picking up more fans worldwide than ever before.
Whitesnake had also re-recorded 'Fool For Your Loving' which again featured as a more 'bluesy' rock standard on the 1980 release 'Ready An' Willing'; the new versions of the classics were dividing the fans.
So, the 1990 performance of Whitesnake had been upstage by the old pro's Aerosmith, who were again on steep curve to renewed success. Whitesnake would return to play as special guests to Def Leppard 19 years later, but we would only had to wait 4 years for the return of Aerosmith, then boosted to the headline position.

"There are two clips from the 1990 which are THE most requested videos on Whitesnake.com; videos from that Monsters Of Rock."
David Coverdale (Whitesnake – Vocals)

"For me it's a personal triumph, I have always been a lover of British Rock'N'Roll .It was always my dream to be in a British band and to Headline a major festival in England where people have come from all corners of the earth."
Rudy Sarzo (Whitesnake – Bass)

"We want to take this time to thank the fans, we had a few technical problems we ironed them out but that shit happens in Rock'N'Roll you know.
For a lot of times shows are consistently tough to do but this wasn't. It was an above average out door show, but hey it takes two to tango and the fans were fantastic."
Brett Michaels (Poison – Vocals)

"Before Donington we were on tour in America and every show on that tour was sold out.
We were never 'glam rock', we were more like 'Steptoe and Son' on speed, it was our gypsy look.
I spent most of the day, before my family turned up, with Jimmy Page, because our tour manager was Richard Cole, who was Led Zeppelin's tour manager. We had been on tour in America and had gone through about four tour managers and I remember that we were in somewhere like Bumfuck, Idaho and I saw this guy and he was pouring a bottle of Jack Daniels down the drain, by a tour bus and then a

bottle of vodka and I said 'what the fuck are you doing?' and it was Richard Cole.

When we played it was very weird watching 70,000 people singing along to your songs in the broad daylight; 'Meet the gangs 'cause the boys are here, the boys to entertain you…..' that was our intro tape.

It's always a good time with the Quireboys and everyone loves a tune that you can whistle.

After Donington they all left and I was left with Thunder; the Thunderbirds were the most embarrassing thing you've seen in your life."
Spike (The Quireboys – Vocals)

"When we came to Donington it was a real event, with 5 or 6 bands and 72,000 people.

When you go into Donington as a band, in a bus, you go over the top of the hill and you could see the audience, this huge audience and that's when you get a daunting feeling. Everyone has probably seen the footage, but when you go up these stairs and you can see from the side of the stage this sea of people, that's when you go 'oh fucking hell'. But luckily enough we were in our early twenties and you have that confidence to go out and do it; I'd probably shit myself now!"
Guy Griffin (The Quireboys – Guitar)

"Donington was very different for us, we had started make some money. We'd recorded an album in LA in '89 and Sharon (Osbourne) was our manager, so by 1990 things had changed quite a lot.

We'd toured at the end of '89 and then again March and we'd also done Top Of The Pops.

We had already played with Aerosmith. We had our dressing room all day, which was different to Reading, so we stayed there all day and had our friends over! The stage was a lot bigger and the crowd was around 77,000.

Playing in daylight was quite bizarre and the wind was blowing you around, which was different as we were used to club dates and we played above Thunder.

We wandered around backstage saying hello to Steven Tyler and Whitesnake. Back then Whitesnake were quite friendly, but we've recently done a tour with them and got thrown off it!"

Nigel Mogg (The Quireboys – Bass)

"The first time we played was quite spectacular and we had a lot riding on it.

We had a few small 'warm up' gigs before Donington and Danny had a throat virus and lost his voice on the tour. It was four days before we were due to play at Donington to 93,500 people and there was a lot of anticipation because the year before it had been cancelled, because of what had happened the year before that and we were opening and it was a really cracking bill.

Danny went to see his Harley Street specialist and he said 'I am going to give you an injection and you mustn't talk for three days', which for Danny is quite difficult.

So he went away and rested and we just sat in corners and worried a lot.

Even the day before we played he wasn't aloud to speak; so we turned up on the day and even he didn't know if anything was going to come out!

We went and sound checked without him. We went out onto this huge stage, in front of this huge field and I was thinking 'I wonder what it's going to look like when it's full of people?' The sound check went nicely and we were still worried about Danny. He still hadn't spoken a word and he had no idea what was going to come out of his throat.

I remember that the stage manager came in and said ½ an hour and we all went quiet, especially Danny! We couldn't get away with all instrumentals; we're not a 'prog rock' band are we!

We turned up on the stage and the first number we were in was 'She's So Fine' and there's one particular note and if he hits that we'd know everything was OK. He hit this note absolutely spot on with laser like precision and if you watch the video of us on one of our DVD's, you can see the look of relief on all of our faces; you could see us all going 'everything's going to be OK.

It was a magical moment and from that point on we were so happy and it came out in our performance and we had one of the best gigs of our life.

It was a great day, really beautiful and sunny.

I couldn't believe how spectacular it was with the field full of arms waving.

At the time we were signed to Capitol records in America and they were really interested in English rock, or in fact, rock music at all.

The president of Capitol at the time said to us that he cursed the day that he signed Poison, who were one of his biggest selling artists at the time.

We were being courted by Geffen Records who had Whitesnake, Guns 'n' Roses, Aerosmith and Cher and just about every good rock band that you cared to mention.

We had a bit of a 'celebrity fan club' at this point and David Coverdale, very kindly, was talking to David Geffen and John Kalodner about us, 'you've got to hear this band Thunder'. Axl Rose was doing the same, he was a big fan; he stopped us in a car park at the Rainbow Bar and Grill (LA), while he was getting mobbed by people and shouting 'you shouldn't be listening to me; these are the boys you should be listening to!!' So he was telling Geffen to listen to our band and Aerosmith were doing the same!

Subsequently when we supported Aerosmith, we found out that on their tour bus, on the way to Donington, Radio One was broadcasting the concert live and they were listening to it on the radio and Joe and Steven were on the tour bus with John Kalodner. They said to him that this was the band that they were telling him about and he said 'well I'm here now, I guess I can check them out', so the fact that we had a particularly good show that day, got us signed to Geffen America and we got off of Capitol/EMI which had never been done before."

Ben Matthews (Thunder - Guitar)

"That was a crucial point in our career, we had started Thunder in 1989 and had gone out and done

a lot of touring the clubs and a few shows with Aerosmith and a few shows with Heart.
We hadn't realised how popular we'd become and on the day all the hands went in the air and we went wow.
It added poignancy as 1989 had been cancelled, when the kids got killed in the crowd, so this had to go well and the promoters were quite nervous and everything was a bit tense.
We were the first band on, the weather was beautiful and as a result of that show our first album went gold and we sold out some shows in the states."
Luke Morley (Thunder – Guitar)

"Danny lost his voice the week before, we had been very busy, we didn't stop."
Harry James (Thunder – Drums)

"I had to go and see a doctor after Nottingham and he told me to take a few weeks off (yeah right).
We had to cancel Friday's London Marquee show which I was upset about but I got through today.
We had the audience clapping and singing along it was tremendous."
Danny Bowes (Thunder – Vocals)

"Last time we played here was interesting back in 1985. We haven't been able to get back due to recording schedules and touring. We are coming back here in October for some shows and maybe we will do Donington next year and really kick you in the ass."
Stephen Pearcy (Ratt – Vocals)

"The promoters once again played it safe with the choice of acts for the 10th Anniversary of the Donington MOR 1990 Thunder and Quireboys provided traditional British Rock at its best whilst Poison had a party atmosphere going down.

Back stage all eyes were on Steve Vai who seemed to have cameras following him everywhere he went. The dude looked so cool but he had competition for the lenses with the one and only Rock Star duo Steve Tyler and Joe Perry of Aerosmith. Meeting those guys in the flesh was a pretty amazing experience and they gave Whitesnake a real run for their money.

We interviewed a lot of the bands for our radio show and everyone was just thrilled the MOR was back.

The first decade of the Monsters Of Rock would set precedence for decades to come. The courage of the promoters, the dedication from the fans and the performances of the artiste on the bill will proudly grace the pages of British rock history.

The Bailey Brothers brought the Monsters Of Rock into the homes of millions of fans across Europe via MTV and those shows are still circulated and enjoyed to this day. The Donington Monsters Of Rock was the jewel in the crown and we were all kings of the Castle at least for a while!"

The Bailey Brothers (Mick & Dez Donington Comperes)

"1990 was the year of big hair at Donington. Everywhere you looked there were masses of backcombed hair-sprayed barnets, skin tight jeans and cowboy boots as Donington went glam for its 10th

birthday party event. To celebrate this event highlights of the day also went out live on Radio 1 for the first time, which gave many a performer the chance to say a few choice words.

The day was bathed in glorious sunshine (surely another Donington first?!), and the day was completely stolen by the days opening band and relative newcomers Thunder. Danny Bowes and his merry men came on and played a complete blinder and by the time they wound their set up with a drawn out 'Dirty Love' they had everyone singing and dancing along like drunken idiots.

The Quireboys followed and while they couldn't match the euphoria brought to the day by Thunder, they played a solid set and were well received.

Poison hit the stage next and seemed to split the crowd, with those like myself deciding it was more fun to throw bits of melon and any other bits of available rubbish at the band and at others, than put up with their cheesy brand of glam.

Aerosmith got the place jumping again and their set also featured one of the finest collaborations in Donington history when Jimmy Page strolled out onto the stage to join Aerosmith for a blistering performance of 'Train kept a Rollin'.

Once Aerosmith finished it was all downhill from then, with David Coverdale's new version of Whitesnake featuring guitar hero Steve Vai providing a pretty awful performance to finish the day on a downer.

Whitesnake are one of this countries finest exports of blues rock, and with Steve Vai widdling his 'cosmic tapestries' over classic blues rock numbers most were left wondering what the fuck was going on.

Time was even given to nearly every band member to bore the crowd with drawn out solo spots and the crowd started to thin out as people decided a more fun way to end the day was to drink themselves to oblivion while devouring some legendry Donington death burgers.

While standing waiting for the appearance of Aerosmith a fellow punter in front of me decided to have a fag. While sparking up his lighter Aerosmith came onto the stage and the crowd surged forward pushing him and his naked lighter flame into the woman stood directly in front of him. Due to the copious amounts of hairspray on this poor woman's hair the naked flame ignited her hair which went up quicker than Gary Glitter outside a primary school.

The woman was still completely oblivious to this fact until everyone behind her started to throw beer over her to douse the flames. This of course inflamed the matter even more as she turned around and started throwing punches completely unaware why she was the target for everyone to throw beer at. Someone soon managed to let her know her hair was on fire as people continued to throw any available liquid over her head until the flames finally went out, leaving her with a badly smelling, black crispy hair do."

Nigel Taylor (Plymouth)

"My first Donington experience was in 1990. First up were Thunder, the sun was beating down and Danny Bowes belted out those songs, what a voice! I still remain a fan to this day. Next up were the Quireboys they whipped up the crowd good and proper, I recall an inflatable Newkie

Brown bottle or two bouncing around the crowd; I'm thinking Spike probably appreciated this... Later the mighty Aerosmith and Tyler back in the day, when he could still back flip across the stage, what a set list topped off by Jimmy Page. Then Whitesnake, Coverdale's vocals and Steve Vai's guitar just completed the day's hard rockin' goodness. I remember getting back home in the wee small hours thinking that it just doesn't get any better than this..." **Matt Allison (Plymouth)**

"I went to Donington Monsters Of Rock festival in 1990. I was eighteen years of age.
Whilst there I was hit, with considerable force, by a passing tennis ball.
It hurt."
Mrs Holly Allison (nee Taylor as I was then, Plymouth)

"1989 was cancelled while the powers that be decided on the future of the festival after the tragedies of '88.
I was quite relieved when they announced that 1990 would go ahead, this was the correct response, learn from the lessons, implement the changes and get on with it. I think that cancelling indefinitely would have had a disastrous effect on all major outdoor music events.
So line-up released (surprisingly only 5 bands this year) it was time to dust of the cordial containers and head off to sunny Derbyshire again. I must admit that Aerosmith aside, I was not overly excited by that years line-up and considered it to be somewhat

weaker than the previous two, however, this was Monsters of Rock and I would have probably attended if the Wurzels were headlining, just being there and soaking up the atmosphere was enough for me at that time.

It was noticeable on entering the arena that the crowd was considerably less than '88 and was back to a more manageable size, this was way better and meant that you could actually visit the stalls at the back again without the risk of losing the crowd you were with.

Thunder were today's openers and were well received by most of the early day crowd, our group included. They played all of their radio friendly hits from what was easily their best album ever, the sublime 'Backstreet Symphony' and left us in jovial spirits, a great party band and possibly the best opening performance of any band at MOR.

I was not a fan of the Quireboys so their set largely passed me by, they seemed to get on ok and got away without being bombarded with too many missiles. I thought that they were a bit of a come down after Thunders sing-a-long set.

Poison were the first of only two American bands on that day, this was weird and in complete contrast to '87 where all of the acts were from the states. Poison were a bit of a marmite band, you either loved them or would prefer to stick your head in a barrel of acid than subject your ears to their poodle haired sounds. I fell into the former category but I also refused to fall into the silly thrash vs. glam nonsense that was prevalent at the time, I liked both.

I remember Poison's set being somewhat unremarkable and suffering from a sound mix that was being carried away by the slightest gust and completely drowned out by the usual low flying 737's. Apart from the usual enthusiastic first ten rows, the crowd seemed to react lethargically to their set and it passed; not threatening to go into the list of legendary Donington performances.

On that day, Aerosmith could have played anything they wanted and I would have been hooked. It was my first chance to see the Toxic Twins who were at that point in time, within my top five favs. I was hooked from the off, Steven Tyler with white and black scarved mic in tow ran about the stage like a man possessed as they went through mostly newer stuff early on but for me it was the trio of 'Sweet Emotion', 'Toys In The Attic' and 'Dream On' that got me really singing along. And then to top it off in style, Jimmy Page joined them for an incredible encore of 'Train Kept A Rollin' and 'Walk This Way'.

Bottle fights occurred as usual, as did peoples liking for recreating Egypt's finest monuments but I do not remember either activity being as prominent as previous years. In fact I fail to remember witnessing any event that was particularly odd or outrageous. Where were the naked sports people, fire starters or Hells Angels tipping over burger vans? Maybe they were all there but I managed to miss them all.

I was not particularly looking forward to Whitesnake, apart from a handful of tracks. I did not care for their recorded material, even more so since they had ditched their better blues style in favour of a more commercial hair band, widdly diddly, and power ballad mad style. What's more, I could not stand David Coverdale, his pompous, big headed, patronising attitude got right on my tits. That said, I did not hate their performance that night and even sang along to the tracks that I could bear. Their sound mix was top notch and the majority of the crowd responded enthusiastically. This set was going out live on BBC1 albeit with several seconds delay to help remove any foul language! Coverdale responded to this accordingly and was deliberately littering the set with as many 'Fucks' as he could muster between and during songs, I believe that a few got through which must have had the good old Beeb fuming.

Although I do not consider 1990 as being one of the better lineups, I remember it as the most relaxing of these fests. The mood was friendly as usual, the weather was pretty warm and the drink flowed well; most importantly we had lots of fun and it was great to have the festival back, it could have been taken away from us for good!"

Roger Moore (Glinton, Peterborough)

"Only five bands this year and the headline slot saw the return of (the now) MTV friendly Whitesnake. Their traditional blues rock had been sidelined for a sleeker USA style heavy metal.

Their show was based around the 'Slip of the Tongue' CD and just didn't excite me like the days of old……the only real nod to the past was a perfunctory version of 'Ain't No Love In The Heart Of The City'. David Coverdale's voice had also lost some of its magic.

Disappointing to say the least.
Aerosmith hadn't played these shores for a while, so they were eagerly anticipated. They didn't disappoint, even Jimmy Page joined them onstage for the encore. Band of the day…..easily.
Poison could have done better, but at least they played 'Every Rose Has Its Thorn', which my wife (whose name is Rose) enjoyed.
Not too sure that The Quireboys were right for the show, but they entertained a sizeable portion of the crowd, so who am I to complain.
Thunder were fantastic. From the moment Danny opened his mouth at the start of 'She's So Fine' to the end of 'Dirty Love'. I was near the front and thought they were great…..best opening performance of all the Doningtons.
The whole concert was broadcast live all day on Radio One.
The weather was fine.
Also this was one of the first years where alcohol had affected my recollections of the day."
Paul Hartshorn (Chesterfield)

1991
AC/DC

Metallica, Motley Crue, Queensrÿche, The Black Crowes

This year would be mostly dominated by two major facts,
1) AC/DC were playing again and the appearance would be their 3rd headline slot within the 12 festivals career span so far.
2) Metallica had gradually risen from the mid-afternoon slot, to now being in the 'special guest' position, playing just before the headliner.

First on were The Black Crowes, a slightly random choice for Donington, but as the festival encompassed 'all that was rock', why shouldn't they play?

With 'Shake Your Money Maker' released the previous year, the majority of the crowd were aware of or absolutely loved, the tracks played on the day. Getting an airing from the album were many of the gems that had made the album a multi platinum seller in their native USA, these included 'Twice As Hard', 'Hard To Handle' and 'Jealous Again'.

Next on were Queensrÿche. More suited to the atmospheric conditions of a dark club gig, Queensrÿche lost some of their aura in the open field in the middle of the afternoon, but still put on a great show. Playing tracks from their astounding 1988 concept album 'Operation Mindcrime' and the 1990 release 'Empire', they showed the crowd how 'progressive metal' could be done, polished, note perfect and hard hitting.

Coming back for their 2nd appearance at Donington were Motley Crue, seven years after their opening slot debut and 6 months before Vince Neil would leave the band.

The album 'Dr. Feelgood' had been released in 1989 and had been a multi platinum success, but there would be no more Crue albums until 94's 'Motley Crue' which would feature John Corabi (ex of The Scream) on lead vocals; Motley Crue were a band in turmoil.

Playing tracks from most of their previous albums, with the exception of 'Theatre Of Pain', they included a cover of 'Anarchy In The UK' as the final track of the set.

Metallica were on next and it was only 5 days after the release of the 'Black Album', which would see them rise to stadium and festival headliners within the year.

The set featured 'Enter Sandman' and 'Sad But True' from the new album and tracks from their whole back catalogue plus the usual two covers.

At the time Metallica had been on a major support tour with AC/DC so they seemed the obvious choice to be in the 'special guest' spot at Donington and they certainly now were something special.

AC/DC returned for their 3rd top of the bill; we would have to wait another 19 years before they returned to headlining Download 2010, making them the band that has headlined equally the most times at Donington with Iron Maiden.

With a set featuring all the best songs from their career, the show was released as the video (then DVD and now Blu-Ray) 'Live At Donington', featuring cannons, inflatables and the giant 'Hells Bell'.

AC/DC were a band at the top of their game, with continuing success and still churning out platinum albums. The ultimate singalong rock band, with more hits and well known tracks than most headliners AC/DC had created a legacy at Donington.

"We were doing a whole run with AC/DC and it was right when the 'Black Album' was coming out in

August of 1991 and we were doing about six or seven weeks with AC/DC and it was just amazing.
We had started fourth from the bottom, then third and then second on the bill.
We were on before AC/DC, we'd had Motley Crue on before us and 'Enter Sandman' had just come out. You could just feel the whole thing was about to go to the next level; there was just a confidence and excitement in the air that was exciting.
We played two new songs from the 'Black Album', 'Enter Sandman' and 'Sad But True' and they went down well and we were just young and 'full of spunk' and going for it big time, definitely feeling confident and getting ready to play the 'big league'.
It was just great to be part of the AC/DC thing and get to watch them every night. I'd go and behind Chris Slade and watch them every night; hanging around AC/DC for six weeks was just amazing. Once in a while I would get invited to have a cup of tea with Angus which was so amazing. We would share our rock 'n' roll lives, which was very cool; also having Motley Crue there was very cool, because it meant that there was definitely a debaucherous element there at all times. It was a great late summer."
Lars Ulrich (Metallica – Drums)

"*It was pretty much socialising with the other bands; we did some interviews and then got up and played. From the band stand point, they are all pretty much the same; some have better food and better trailers, but usually not.*
Well this time it wasn't raining which was a kind of a change.

A lot of times there are the paying audience and the ones that are just there to watch; it's better for everyone when the crowd just lets themselves go. We like the people in the audience to bond in a way that's really beyond words; it's one of those things that's indescribable and it goes across all countries, social, political, religious, you name it!
It's very mystical and beyond language and you really feel that at some festivals where the audience is really 'there'. I do feel that the media is based on a 'sports model', but concerts aren't based on that model and it's hard to score.
So, of all the gigs that we have done in our career, the gigs that really stand out for me the most are the ones where the people are really letting themselves experience it and that's a great feeling.
One thing that I like about Donington is that they tend to have a more eclectic type of bill."
Geoff Tate (Queensrÿche – Vocals)

"*In my opinion, 1991 had a very strong, diverse line-up that in theory should have kept everybody happy. We had the new raw sound of Pantera, the bluesy swagger of The Black Crowes, some modern Prog rock from Queensryche, Motley Crue for the glam / sleaze crowd, the ever growing beast called Metallica supplying the Thrash and last but not least, the mighty AC/DC racking up their third (and final) headline slot.*
I was happy as the proverbial sand boy when I saw that line-up in Kerrang! and hurriedly collected some tickets from our local ticket shop (which disappeared soon after the emergence of the internet). We had six

bands this year again and August could not come around quick enough.

By now we considered ourselves veterans and had the whole thing down to a fine art! We travelled light but still had adequate provisions to last us all day, we were also prepared for all potential August weather conditions. Every year at least one festival virgin would join us and despite continual reminders of what to take, they would always come ill prepared. My girlfriend Sue's friend joined us one year and insisted on wearing high heel shoes, this was a decision that she would later regret as they sank in the mud constantly as she trudged slowly around the toilet blocks.

Pantera were an emerging force to be reckoned with and they hit the stage like an uncaged tiger, their sound was brutal with riffs that could skin cattle at 200yds. I was only just getting into them at this time and only new the odd track from 'Vulgar Display of Power' such as 'Walk', however, this performance was suitably impressive enough to encourage me to buy the two albums they had released so far. It was noticeable again that there were very few bottles heading in Panteras direction, maybe people were just too scared of Phil Anselmo and did not wish to be on the receiving end of some five knuckle retribution .As expected Sue hated every minute of their set.

The Black Crowes were about as far removed from Pantera as it could possibly get, their sound was more southern blues but they kicked ass in their own way and were always entertaining to watch. Their 'Shake Your Money Maker' album was riding high in the rock charts and they belted out energetic versions of 'Twice As Hard' and the big hit of the time 'Jealous Again' to an appreciative audience.

Queensryche were at that time (and for at least a decade after) myself and Sue's favourite band. We had witnessed them at Hammersmith Odeon twice and they had put in fantastic performances playing 90% of 'Operation Mindcrime' with the entire crowd singing along to every word. As an indoor live band they were one of the best out there and always gave 200%. Unfortunately it quickly became apparent to us that the energy and atmosphere they created indoors could not be recreated in an outdoor environment, it just did not seem to work and was a sad experience for us. The band did not play badly and Geoff Tate's vocals were as brilliant as ever, there was just something missing which was not helped by the set list which was less than inspiring and the crowd did not really warm to them on that occasion. Thankfully, we have seen them countless times after this and they have been superb every time.

As far as I can remember the weather remained good all day but to be honest the weather was rarely that bad and if there was a downpour it never lasted particularly long. On most occasions I did not need to dig out the trusty bin liners, and if I did it was usually for seating purposes which is the preferred option over sitting on chips and Chinese noodles.

It was Motley Crue's second appearance at the festival but this time around they were for obvious reasons much higher up the bill. The Crue were another band that you either loved or hated, the Thrash Fans in the audience would absolutely despise them but I loved them. I will never fathom out *why some people get into this mentality of dissing particular styles of music which are effectively in the same genre, if you don't like it don't listen to it and let us who want to , do so in peace.*

Apart from Mick Mars (as usual), the Crue were full of energy and treated us to some choice cuts from 'Dr Feelgood', 'Girls Girls Girls' etc but from my vantage point they were not going down as well as they had in '84, the crowd was receptive but not overly enthusiastic. Vince Neil has never been the greatest vocalist in the world but gets by well enough and is well suited to their style, on this occasion he seemed to be having a problem reaching all of the notes which probably added to the crowds mostly lethargic reception. That said, the crowd got moving a bit more for the set closer, a decent version of 'Anarchy In The UK'.

In '91 it was becoming apparent that Metallica would soon be the biggest metal band on the planet. The pioneers of thrash were starting to lose many die hard fans after the release of the 'Black Album' but on this sunny August afternoon they were still kings of the hill in many peoples eyes. Their last opus 'And Justice For All' had sold bucket loads but was not held in as high regard as its predecessor 'Master Of Puppets' but still had some killer cuts such as my all time favourite 'One' and a large proportion of the masses in attendance (Glam die hards aside) were well up for this performance. Wearing the traditional black against a black backdrop James and the crew pummelled us into early submission with new and soon to be most famous track 'Enter Sandman' then another favourite of mine 'Creeping Death'. Other highlights included 'Fade to Black', 'Master Of Puppets', 'Seek And Destroy', 'One' and finally a brutal headbangers favourite 'Battery'.

I do not see the need to wax lyrical about AC/DC's performance, proof of how good they were that night is available for all to see in the form of the Video (or DVD in the techy modern world) that they shot of the entire performance. When I watched this video several years later I was glad that it captured the show just how I remember it. I could not fault the show or performances that night, it was the last time that I saw DC and if I do not witness them again at least I can whack in the DVD for a quick refresher of them at their peak.

We travelled down by minibus again that year and of course had to cough up the usual ridiculous fee so that we could wait for hours before we actually got out of the car park. This waiting time was usually spent blasting out the stereo, which of course everybody else was also doing in their vehicles making the din somewhat undecipherable. During this wait at some point everybody would need the use of a WC which of course was not provided in the car park, therefore any old tree or car tyre (or bush in the case of the ladies) would have to succumb to our urinal needs. Car tyres seemed to be the prime choice of one of my regular colleagues, I don't know what it was but he seemed to have a thing for them, this proved dangerous on several occasions as several of the vehicles were occupied at the time, on one occasion an Oak tree sized biker type jumped out of his land rover to remonstrate with our pissing *friend but luckily was calmed down before face punching could commence.*

In '90 I remember that my brother got out of the van via the back door to relieve himself just as we were able to actually move, therefore we decided that it would be a fun game to drive off and stop about 50 yds away, this of course became the age old fun game of "lets wait for him to catch up then drive off again" we continued this game for at least ten minutes, It is amazing how childish games can keep you occupied in such circumstances, the atmosphere at festivals does have that effect on people though."
Roger Moore (Glinton, Peterborough)

"This was the first time our now depleted gang had not travelled down in our own transport. Instead we caught the train to Derby, then the organised shuttle bus service to the site. At the end of the show we did it all in reverse.

1991 saw the most impressive stage show of them all, with AC/DC having twenty-one cannons lined up across the top of the stage.

This was the best (by far) of the three AC/DC headlining shows at Donington, culminating in a very loud 21-gun salute at the end of 'For Those About to Rock'.

Angus also performing his guitar solo spot on top of a podium in the middle of the crowd during 'Let There Be Rock'

One of the best Donington shows ever.

Supporting 'DC was Metallica, who with the release of their 'Black' album had suddenly leapt into the mainstream of rock. From a personal point of view

their new direction suited my musical taste buds at the time. I went on to enjoy all of their 90s material and concerts.
Another big name on the bill in 1991 was Motley Crue, to be honest not exactly my cup of tea, so I don't remember much about their performance.
Queensryche & Black Crowes were also on the bill."
Paul Hartshorn (Chesterfield)

1992
Iron Maiden
Skid Row, Thunder, Slayer, WASP, The Almighty

Iron Maiden headlined Donington 1992 for their 2nd time; in 2003 they would return again for their 3rd appearance and making it the 4th time in 2007,

smashing the record set by AC/DC and Metallica. AC/DC will equal this record with their 4th headline appearance in 2010.
The performance by Iron Maiden was recorded for the video and double cd, called 'Live At Donington'.

Iron Maiden are one of the three bands that are most recognised as 'Donington Icons', the other two being Metallica and AC/DC. Who can forget the battle cry of Bruce Dickinson cutting through the night air as he yells 'SCREAM FOR ME DONINGTON'.

The Almighty, who opened the day, also recorded their set for a future cd release. A hard rocking set from 'north of the border' was just what was needed to blow away the cobwebs and clear the heads, that were already topping up with the first pints of alcohol of the day. Ricky Warwick, the lead singer of the Almighty, would make his solo debut at Download Festival in the tent, playing his 'Americana' based solo music, 11 years later in 2003.

Back for a second appearance, W.A.S.P. played another good selection of tunes from their back catalogue, including their latest album 'The Crimson Idol', but they were not as threatening and exciting as the were the first time that they played, though their career has had great longevity and they are due another appearance.

Slayer were making their very first appearance at the festival in '92 and it was also their first appearance since Dave Lombardo had left; their new drummer, Paul Bostaph, had previously

played with Forbidden. Slayer were the last of the 'Big Four' to play Donington. The Big Four were Metallica, Anthrax, Slayer and Megadeth and it referred to the main players in the world of thrash metal. Of the four bands, Slayer were the most aggressive, with the most controversial songs included songs like 'Angel Of Death' and "Raining Blood'. An excellent set, by the masters of 'Satanic thrash'.
Thunder were back for their second appearance in 2 years and had risen up the line-up from openers to 3rd from top. Another solid classic rock set, Thunder always delivered and were again a very popular performer on the day. Skid Row were special guests on the day and very deserving of the position. Having played as the opening band at the Bon Jovi Milton Keynes show in 1999, their increasing popularity, mostly due to their enigmatic frontman Sebastian Bach. With a set featuring all their most popular songs from '18 And Life' and 'Youth Gone Wild' to newer ones like 'Monkey Business' and the set opener 'Slave To The Grind', Skid Row were the slightly less crazy GNR and their frontman was a much better singer than Axl, these were a band on the way up.
So it was up to the mighty 'Maiden' to finish the day off and they did in grand style; a British band blasting out their many hits to an adoring crowd of denim and leather clad metal heads. They wouldn't return to the hallowed grounds of Donington for another eleven years.

"In 1992 it pissed down with rain, which is always a bit difficult for an audience at a festival, it doesn't get them in the best possible mood.
It was a couple of days before our second album. I think the bill wasn't as good that year as when we did it in '90 it was Whitesnake and Aerosmith and it was a difficult bill for Thunder to be on with Maiden and Slayer, but god bless our punters, despite it pissing down with rain, it was a good day"
Luke Morley (Thunder – Guitar)

"The second time was good fun as we were further up the bill, which was a lot nicer, but it was pissing down with rain, which is a nightmare.
It's really difficult playing in the rain, as it doesn't come straight down and blows in your face, all over your hands, all over your fret board, all over the stage, all over your leather boots and I remember Sebastian Bach slipped over twice; he came flying out, said 'hello Donington' and fell flat on his ass!
The weather definitely put a bit of a damper on it.
Playing in the driving rain is very difficult; it plays havoc with your hair as well!!
It's a very important festival. It has served us very well indeed and a lot of the press said that we were the best band of the day."
Ben Matthews (Thunder - Guitar)

"August 22nd 1992 was a huge day for me because Donington was the 'Holy Grail' of metal. It was just a huge dream come true for me, having been there in

'88. I kept thinking most of the day that I had done it; I had fulfilled one of my dreams to play there.

We opened the show, full of excitement, happy to be there, very nervous and a complete feeling of wanting to do well.

The rest of the day goes into a bit of a blur. We came off, started having a few drinks, hanging out and we started doing interviews. But the actual being on stage I remember really vividally and just looking out at a sea of people, it was just amazing! I wasn't able to get my breath for the first two songs, it was just like 'oh my god, this is just mental!!' Then I started to relax and get into it and before you knew it, it was over.

But in the lead up to it, I remember staying in a hotel the night before and listening to the radio and hearing our name getting mentioned that we were opening it up and then waking up in the morning and knowing that today we were going to open up Donington, for a soccer player it must be like going to a cup final, for us it was like going to a cup final!"
Ricky Warwick (The Almighty – Vocals/Guitar)

"We opened up the show in '92. I had never played to an audience that size before and as soon as we got out there adrenaline just took over; it was easily one of the highlights of my gigging career and I have done thousands and thousands of gigs. Donington and supporting Metallica at Milton Keynes Bowl the year after are pretty much the two best gigs I have ever done.

I remember seeing Tom Araya at the side of the stage smiling, which was cool.

We didn't get to see much of the other bands as we were stuck in a portakabin doing interviews for most of the day and by the time we got out it was pretty much done and dusted. But we managed to watch Maiden and also saw a tiny bit of Skid Row and they had the worse weather of the day."
Pete Friesen (The Almighty – Guitar)

*"Little did I know that 11 years later I would be playing bass in the opening band?
Our agent John Jackson had our dressing-portakabin loaded with Huggies and talc. Thankfully they weren't needed."*
Floyd London (The Almighty – Bass)

*"What I do remember was that Tommy Vance was going to introduce us on stage, but when they tried to get us on stage, he decided he wasn't going to. So we had to get our man Bomber to do it, the same guy who introduced us on the live Album; 'Donington can I welcome to the stage, the All Loud, All Wild, the All Fuckin' Mighty'; he did that at the last minute, as he was forced to do it.
All the stuff hat I had thought about before about being calm went out the window and I played 'Crucify' at twice the speed it should have been!
We were the first and usually the first band doesn't get much of a reaction, but the whole crowd was there and we got one of the best reactions, apart from the headliners of course.
We had just come back from Australia at the time and it was great to get that amount of cheers.*

After that, the set was a blur. There were lots of Scotland flags being waved and lots of cheering.
Then we went backstage and I met Steve Harris and Sebastian Bach and it just went downhill from there and there's not much more I can remember."
Stump 'Stumpy' Monroe (The Almighty – Drums)

"I have one odd memory from before 3 Colours Red... I was drunkenly stumbling around the festival in '92 when a girl randomly stopped me and asked for a photograph, don't ask me why... but I'm like, "erm, ok then!"
That to me is what the festival is about; the crowd is friendly and always really pissed! I don't know how many times I've walked around the crowd trying not to step on hung-over rock fans asleep clutching a bottle of their own piss! Donington rules, shits all over Glastonbury because it is rock, and we all know that rock has the best fans and the best music."
<u>Pete Vuckovic</u> (3 Colours Red – Vocals/Bass)

"I don't think I ever saw anybody's set in all those years; I was always too busy running around backstage. I do remember, though, being in the photo pit for Slayer's sound check one year....let's just say it was a life-changing experience!"
Judy Totton (Monsters Of Rock PR)

"I was a teenager when I first went to Donington in 1992. My friend and I went on a coach trip to Monsters Of Rock, which was headlined by Iron

Maiden that year. I remember being SO excited to be in the same field as Skid Row!"
Emma Watson (PR – Bowling For Soup/MC Lars/Zebrahead)

"My best memories of Donington Park go way back to 1992 when the festival was still called 'Monsters Of Rock' and the mighty Iron Maiden were headlining for a second time.
There was such an awesome bill that day with British upstarts The Almighty kicking off the day quickly followed by W.A.S.P., Slayer, Thunder and Skid Row as special guests.
I remember this festival most as this was my first ever gig and I would be seeing my favourite band Iron Maiden and I pretty much liked every band that was appearing that day.
The campsite was an awesome experience, something I didn't expect. We got together with a bunch of guys from 'up north' who had accidentally burnt their tent down and we had this huge tent so we offered them part of it for the weekend. One of the guys from what I remember was a Dave Mustaine look alike and had passed out quite early on in the night.
When I finally dragged myself into the tent for some sleep I found myself quickly awakened by the constant taking off and landing of the planes overhead. The next morning I woke up and the guy was still dead to the world, everyone else was awake so I gave him a shove to see if he wanted a beer. When he woke up I said to him 'how the hell did you sleep through the racket of the planes and the car

stereos blasting out throughout the night?'; at this point he tucked his hair behind his ears and proceeded to turn on his hearing aids, I felt like such a tool, I didn't even realise.

The best memories of the gig were Skid Row front man Sebastian Bach's impressive stage dive at the start of the set when he went arse over tit from all the rain, but they played an impressive set and witnessing probably one of Iron Maidens finest shows, which I relive on DVD regularly and the loudness of 72,000 people singing every word in unison."

Neil & Maria Bees (Perth, Australia)

"Iron Maiden returned to show the world they could still cut it. And cut it they did, although I must admit to being very drunk by the time they came on stage.

After the fireworks had finished we made our way through the exits with the rest of the crowd, but for some reason I decided to run up a grass bank, only to lose my balance and fall heavily back down to the bottom. Several minutes later I was in the back of an ambulance on my way to Derby Royal Infirmary with a dislocated thumb.

The pain sobered me up somewhat.

The embarrassing part then was to telephone my eight month pregnant wife at four in the morning to come to collect me. I didn't get much sympathy.

I don't know whether it was my musical tastes changing or the rock world in general (I blame Nirvana and the whole grunge movement) but from 1992 onwards the Donington line ups weren't exciting me as much as they used to. Don't get me wrong, I

was still enjoying the whole atmosphere and the day out, but looking back in hindsight is that all it was towards the end….just a good day out.
Skid Row, Slayer, WASP just came and went
Even Thunder just weren't as impressive as they had been two years earlier, maybe I had seen them too many times in a short period of time (five or six times within the last twelve months).
1992 had been memorable, but not necessarily for the right reasons.
Once again their was a hiatus the following year. Maybe this would recharge the festivals and my batteries."
Paul Hartshorn (Chesterfield)

1994
Aerosmith
Extreme, Sepultura, Pantera, Therapy? Pride and Glory

2nd Stage:
The Wildhearts
Terrorvision, Skin, Biohazard, Cry of Love, Headswim

After a break of a year, Monsters Of Rock returned in '94, this year with the addition of a 2nd stage featuring smaller popular rock and metal bands.

The second stage featured British favourites Terrorvision, Skin and The Wildhearts in the headline position. The Wildhearts came back to play Download in 2008, Skin played the mainstage in 2009; Terrorvision have yet to return to Donington. Headswim, Cry Of Love and Biohazard also played; Biohazard had their set cut short after two songs when they overly encouraged the crowd to come on stage and there was a massive stage invasion.

Pride & Glory were the first band on the mainstage, a band that featured Ozzy's guitarist Zakk Wylde on lead guitar; this band was the band that Zakk formed before Black Label Society where he would see much more success.

Therapy? were on next and this would be their first of four appearances. Gaining chart success since the release of their most popular album 'Troublegum' in February 1994, the set was popular, though they were not a normal type of MOR band. Over the next year there popularity would increase even more with the release of 'Infernal Love' and they would be back to fill the 'special guest slot'.

Next was a 'double whammy' of extreme metal in the shape of Pantera from the US and Sepultura from Brazil; but to follow this with the soft rock of

Extreme, playing hits such as 'More Than Words' was a bizarre choice. The metal fans wanted thrashing metal and what they got was the popular radio sounds of Gary Cherone and the boys from Massachusetts, a lot of the fans in front of the mainstage weren't happy.

But most people were happy with the final band, Aerosmith were back now in top slot and four years since they had supported Whitesnake at Donington.

Steven Tyler and Joe Perry were American music icons and were seen as the American rock version of Keith Richards and Mick Jagger from the Rolling Stones, with a similarly large music selection to back them up. Playing such hits as 'Dude Looks Like A Lady', 'Sweet Emotion' and 'Walk This Way', they had the crowd eating out of their hands and who could not love their style of performing, the back flips, the posing, the playing up to the crowd, they were a massive success.

The return of Aerosmith in 2010 will equal the three headline appearances of Metallica and only Iron Maiden and AC/DC will have headlined more times, with AC/DC's 2010 appearance notching up four top slots and equalling that of Iron Maiden.

"Donington's a weird one. I grew up on punk rock, I was a 'punk kid' and I formed Therapy? with Michael and he was a 'metal kid'.

The people we hung around with, in the small town we're from, 'the outsiders' liked punk and metal,

Ramones, Motorhead, AC/DC and Iron Maiden. But whenever I met anyone from our village that'd been to Donington it was always long hair, cut off denims and patches, which wasn't really my scene.

When Therapy? Started out I was only into Thrash metal and the only metal bands I liked were early Iron Maiden, Motorhead and AC/DC, everything else was a bit too pomp and theatrical and not really what I liked.

The first time we got offered Donington, all I remember was the outrage at the time because we had short hair! A few years ago Metal Hammer did a 'piece' on 'Days That Changed Metal' and one of them was Therapy? played Donington in 1984.

We were second on the mainstage and we had short hair and bands like Skid Row were on. People were thinking 'well Kerrang! has championed the band and you're hear in front of the Metal faithful, but if you go down really badly that will be the decider'! Michael he was up for it and I just went onstage and by the end of the set it was absolutely brilliant.

Troublegum was out then and we'd had a few singles in the charts and then after Donington the album just went up the charts and we did Reading the same year and we got a Gold disc out of it. But, I remember Donington was the most daunting one because the NME had extensively covered the band, so Reading was like a safe bet. But just before Donington Kerrang! had latched onto the band, but we did get letters in asking why we had short hair.

But, I remember the gig being very good and after about 4 songs in thinking this is great and the crowd's fantastic."

Andy Cairns (Therapy? – Vocals/Guitar)

"When we played at Donington, I got out of the van, to have a wee (because I was that excited) before we'd even got in and the van drove off!
For some reason I had my rucksack and my bags for the mainstage and I had to walk in with the crowd and blagged my way past security, telling them that I was playing on the second stage.
I remember standing on the hill and Sepultura had just finished and then everyone came over to the second stage. Considering these people had come from watching Sepultura, to come and watch us, with our 'doo wops' and singing about 'Our House' it was fantastic.
They all put their hands in the air and gave us a taste for more.
It was a bastion of rock!!!
If we had a 'fuckin' brilliant album to come back with, we would come back."

Tony Wright (Terrorvision – Vocals)

"Early 94 saw us break thru into the charts and offers to play both Donington and Reading dropped onto our doormat. How cool was that???? Donington was great 'cos we'd always been there as kids and we were sandwiched between Sepultura and Pantera!"

Leigh Marklew (Terrorvision - Bass)

"Terrorvision played literally thousands of festivals, it's hard for me to distinguish one from another, mainly due to the state I have usually been in at these events. The nineties may have been a blur but

a couple of memories are surfacing through....
Mid nineties, the hardcore/ thrash/ macho thing was happening, circling us (TV) like Apache Indians around a small gathering of fun loving cowboys. This didn't affect us in the slightest; in fact it made us more stubborn about writing pop songs, not only with infectious hook lines, but with longevity too, (as we have recently proved).
So when we played on stage at Donington in between Slayer and Pantera it was quite a feat winning over the audience to the point of them all singing "doo wop" and waving their tattooed arms in the air! Think we got away with that one. Another time we hijacked several golf buggies and rampaged the Donington site, picking up punters here and there, turning them over now and then (buggies not punters). Needless to say there was a Wildheart or two involved as well!"
Mark Yates (Terrorvision – Guitar)

"When Skin was asked to play in 1994 it was a dream come true. The adrenaline was so high at the time I don't remember much about it, but we filmed our video to 'Tower of strength' at Donington so when I watch it, you kind of relive it. When I was thirteen, my sister ran the ZIGZAG club, a venue that held about a thousand people. One particular evening a band called Girl headlined, and at soundcheck there guitarist let me play his Les Paul, and stand on stage and play through his Marshall Stack. That guitarist was Phil Collen, now With Def Leppard, and that day changed my life.

In 2009 Def Leppard are headlining and Skin will be playing on the same stage, same day. Unbelievable."
Myke Gray (Skin – Guitar)

"Donington was an unforgettable experience for me."
Bobby Hambel (Biohazard – Guitar)

"There was no festival in 1993, I cannot for the life of me remember why it was not held as it was originally planned, we were now starting to worry that all was not right in the camp and that our beloved fest would soon come to an end. This festival had for so many years been an exciting regular part of our lives that we assumed that it would be with us forever.
'94 was the first time that the organisers would be experimenting with a second stage, I looked on this idea mostly positively as it could cut out waiting times between bands and allow us to see twice as many. On the minus side, if you wished to see all or most of the bands on the second stage it would limit time for wondering around the stalls, queuing for beer/ toilets etc.
'94 was also the first time that the fest had been held in any other month than June, I did not particularly like this idea as it meant that the headliner would not be playing the majority of their set in darkness, I do not know why it changed but it sucked in my opinion.
We arrived late this year due to not being too bothered about the first few bands on and also bad traffic on the usual approach roads around the airport, in fact we arrived just in time to see Biohazard being kicked off for allowing the crowd to invade the stage, I believe they managed two songs

before the organisers intervened. I cannot say I was too upset with this outcome as I was not and am never likely to be a fan of theirs.

Biohazard were on the new second stage, this was obviously a lot smaller than the main stage and was located at the back of the arena to the left, an ideal location which did not take long to walk too if you were standing at the back or right side of the main stage.

After watching another brutally efficient display from Pantera which was not too dissimilar to their last several years earlier, we headed back to the second stage to catch Skin. My most vivid memory of Skin's set is of the two six and a half foot 'Hair Bear Bunch' look-alikes that kept blocking our view despite us trying to move out of the way, this did not totally ruin the set as the band played a good sing-along set which included good time ditties such as 'Look but Don't Touch', 'Tower of Strength' and their slightly changed cover of EMF's 'Unbelievable'. Skin didn't seem to last too much longer, they produced at least one more album (may have been two but if so I did not hear it) then just seemed to vanish from the scene. Skin reformed to play last years Download and I was surprised by the amount of people who could not remember them, even stranger was that two of them had been standing with us watching them during their '94 performance, memories and fish spring to mind.

Next up were Brazilian Thrash giants Sepultura, none of our group had gotten into this particular take on the genre so the unanimous decision was to take root at the back of the arena and fill our faces. Max and his troupe seemed to go down well and they seemed to be doing what they did well enough but it was just not for me, I could appreciate them musically but have never been a fan of those bands that utilise the Growl/ Grunt/ What the hell is he going on about approach to the vocals.

Not too impressed with the late afternoon lineup of Terrovision and the Wildhearts (who I now love), we decided to make the traditional wonder around the stands. Food stalls have never been a highlight of any festival but I remember them as being worse in the '80's and '90's, the variety was poorer than now but the prices were equally as extortionate. If we could get away with it we never purchased any food from these rip off merchants which was not too bad a ploy with a one day event as long as you took adequate provisions.

The other stalls also had less variety on offer than there is today. Whereas you can now buy anything from a skull on a stick to an inflatable three piece suite, then there was not much more on offer other than the stalls selling Official MOR and Band tour T Shirts and the odd stall selling flags, posters or non souvenir shirts.

Extreme were an odd choice for special guests on the bill that day; they had risen to a fairly lofty level with their 'Pornograffitti' album but had also driven everybody mad with the 'More than Words' acoustic ballad that seemed to be played everywhere you went, the last straw for me was hearing it in a DIY shop one day. So, as the early evening sun shone, Gary, Nuno and the boys tried their best to get a reaction out of a crowd that had largely been listening to harder edged stuff all day. I didn't mind them too much and I thought that they put in a decent energetic performance of some of there harder, funkier tracks like 'Decedance Dance' and 'Get The Funk Out'. That was all ruined of course when they got their stools out for a tortuous version of the dreaded 'More than ....', they lost the crowd completely from then on but gained plenty of plastic receptacles from the 'boo boys'. They were an odd choice for special guests and were always going to be battling against the rabid Sepultura and Pantera fans.

Aerosmith were of course excellent, treating us to the usual greatest hits set with a smattering of tracks from their current long player 'Get a Grip'. It was an exactly what it says on the tin set, Steven danced, twirled and jumped, Joe created his usual cool poses whilst playing faultlessly and the other boys did as they do best, play well but not wonder from their spots very often. I enjoyed it and everybody around us also seemed to also. Aerosmith were at the height of their commercial success and a good choice for headliner, it's a shame they started to lose the plot not long after.

Overall '94 had its high points (Aerosmith and 2 stages) and lows (June date and not the greatest line-up) but it was still a great day out and I would not have missed it for the world."

Roger Moore (Glinton, Peterborough)

"The festival was moved from its usual mid August slot to early June. This didn't improve the weather any….it was bitterly cold.

There were also two stages this year.
On the smaller stage both Cry of Love and Skin both impressed. Skin released their set on a series of CD singles shortly after the show.
Aerosmith returned to headline the main stage. Although not as good as their support slot four years earlier, they still put on a solid show. Due to a lack of late trains home (we were using this option once again…the gang was now down to two stalwarts) we had to miss the last portion of Aerosmiths' show. We could see the fireworks in the distance as we travelled down the Derbyshire country lanes towards the station.
Extreme were OK, but not as good as I had witnessed at the NEC at couple of years earlier.
Other bands such as Pantera and Sepultura were in my opinion amongst the worst bands ever to perform at Donington. The 'new' Donington crowd seemed to think otherwise though and they both went down well. The future didn't look too good through my eyes."
Paul Hartshorn (Chesterfield)

"I have been attending Donington since 84 but something different from the usual carnage occurred in 1994.
Myself and some friends had been watching a very enjoyable set from the band Cry Of Love on the second stage and decided to chill out at the rear of the main arena when Kelly (?) the lead singer of COL walked by so we called him over for a chat and to congratulate him on a good set.
Kelly sat down and chewed the fat for a while and then noticed one of our group, a mad man by the

name of Eastie, was chugging away on a 5ltr drink container full of a dark sticky liquid. Kelly decided he would ask Eastie for a swig, Eastie duly obliged and told Kelly it would put hairs on his chest. Unbeknown to Kelly the dark sticky liquid was a mix of vodka, southern comfort, whiskey & jack Daniels! Kelly took a good swig, his eyes went as wide as dinner plates his skin turned green and foolishly he tried to stand and walk off nonchalantly........ hence the never forgotten sight of an American rock singer staggering sideways down the hill making excuses that he had to meet someone back stage!
Hilarious and one of many fond memories of the Monsters of rock."
Simon Rucastle (Carnforth)

1995
Metallica

Therapy?, Skid Row, Slayer, Slash's Snakepit, White Zombie, Machine Head, Warrior Soul, Corrosion of Conformity

This year the second stage had disappeared and the festival had another name; instead of MOR it was re-named by the headliners Metallica as 'Escape From The Studio' as they were taking a break from the studio, whilst recording 'Load'.

First on was some 'old school thrash' from Corrosion Of Conformity, favourites of Metallica and then followed by the whacked out 'Acid Punk' rock of Warrior Soul.

Machine Head made their first of many appearances at the Donington site and left quite an impression on the people who caught all of their set. This was a band that had 'staying power' and are now headlining arena shows in their own right across the UK, 15 years later.

The eerie 'horror metal' of White Zombie would have always been a popular choice on the day; the return of Rob Zombie is still eagerly awaited and the Download festival forums are always full of people requesting that Rob plays every year. White Zombie made the most of their short trip to the UK and played Donington on the Saturday, following it up with an appearance at the Reading Festival on the Sunday.

The return to Donington by Slash was a popular choice to watch in the mid afternoon slot and was a lot less eventful than the Guns N' Roses appearance in 1988 when the crowd disaster had struck. Slash's Snake Pit was a bluesier band and really just a vehicle for the guitar skills of Mr Hudson himself. Slash would return again in 2005 & 2007 with Velvet Revolver, a more popular band and a proper group, including Scott Weiland of Stone Temple Pilots on vocal duties.

Slayer made their 2nd appearance in the same spot on the bill as they had occupied 3 years before. Slayer did exactly what it said on the tin, thrash, thrash, quality thrash.

Skid Row were back again this time one position below the guest slot , but still an incredibly popular choice, with an extremely vigorous and energetic performance. Sebastian Bach was still with the band and when they lost him the main focus of the band was gone, though the amazing songs were still there as a testament to their once greatness.

Therapy? had now risen to the 'special guest' slot and even had a cello player, something that wouldn't be seen at Donington until the debut of Apocalyptica in 2003.

Metallica were back to headline the festival for the first time and they were now a band that was unstoppable and musical world domination seemed to be the name of the game.

Playing some of the most precise thrash that had ever graced the stage at the festival, Metallica were such a popular choice most of the people in attendance.

Metallica would be back to headline for the 2nd time in 2004, followed by their 3rd slot in 2006.

So, another Monsters Of Rock had finished, but we didn't know that the following year would be the festivals Swansong; the end of an era, the end of the line, final orders etc. Monsters Of Rock was coming to an end and a much needed different brand of festival would be needed to fill the gap, this would happen with the beginning of Download in 2003, 8 years later.

"Metallica headlines Donington 1995!!!

We were in the middle of the recording of 'Load' and took a break from the studio to come over and play Donington. I think we played a warm up show underneath the Astoria, in the Astoria 2; it was the first time that we played a couple of the songs that ended up being 'Devil Dance' and '2 x 4' that ended up on 'Load' and 'Re-Load'.

It was great to get out of the studio and it was obviously great to headline Donington. It was a very relaxing day; I remember that whenever we played Donington, we were always wound up and nervous and kinda all over the place, but I remember that there was a really calm atmosphere backstage. I remember that we were just hanging out talking to Sebastian Bach and Kerry King and it was just a really effortless day. Everyone was in a good mood and there were no dramas.

We opened up with 'Breadfan' and we played two new songs and we got do a full 2 ½ hour set; it was an incredible day.

Afterwards we went for a 'piss up' down in Birmingham at Edwards Number Eight club. I remember that all the Metallica guys, the Skid Row and Slayer guys 'caravanned' down to Birmingham; we were off the freeway, or the motorway as you call it and we had all been drinking beers and everybody had to piss. We literally stopped somewhere outside of Birmingham, it could have been Wolverhampton or somewhere and the guys from Slayer, Skid Row and Metallica got out and all just started 'peeing' on some guys lawn. We were standing there at 2 o'clock in the morning on the way to the 'After Donington Piss Up

Party' and we were all pissing on some guy's lawn in a suburb of Birmingham, it was quite funny."
Lars Ulrich (Metallica – Drums)

"Metallica were playing Donington as a 'comeback gig' and they've got a more hardcore fan base that like Metallica and nothing else, so it was a lot more difficult for us.
We had a cellist onstage with us at this point, as we'd brought out 'Infernal Love' it had gone Gold and sold a lot of records and we were second from top.
I remember the first half of the set was a lot more difficult because it was Metallica and they weren't really 'indie friendly' and we were in that cult kind of thing, straddling both camps.
It came to opening for Metallica and we'd sold all these records around the world and we opened with the cellist onstage and the Joy Division cover of "Isolation". I remember being conscious for the first few songs that this could go either way.
There was a hardcore of Metallica fans down the front giving us really bad looks. We kind of managed to pull it off towards the end, but it was a lot more nerve-racking than '94. People who were fourteen or fifteen absolutely loved it.
I think a lot of the 'old guard' had been put out of joint by the like of 'Troublegum' and Faith No More, Helmet and Grunge and the fact that we had short hair.
I do remember that it got a lot more corporate for us and we had a big promotional tent backstage and we were whisked 'from pillar to post' doing lots more

interviews, but at the end of the day the gig was still fantastic."
Andy Cairns (Therapy? – Vocals/Guitar)

"WAKE UP!!!! You've got five minutes to get on stage!" was the first thing I heard that day.
We had fallen asleep in the tour bus late the night before, and no one had bothered to wake up me or Rob that morning at Donington. Although we were in the middle of the line up that afternoon, it was afternoon, and time to perform. We threw on some clothes, and were immediately whisked on stage – no coffee, no warm-up, and only the biggest, most important show ever! Talk about an adrenaline o.d. – waking up to so many thousands of people – it was amazing!
We had the unusual title of being the first band ever to play Donington and Reading back to back, which many bands would covet but made us extremely nervous. What if the metalheads thought we were too alternative, and vice versa at Reading? We had heard nightmarish stories about how the British fans might react – bottles of piss hurled at you, sharpened coins, you name it. It was nerve wracking, walking out on to that stage. Especially jolted awake just seconds earlier.
Of course the crowd was fantastic, and it definitely is in the top 3 White Zombie shows ever. Someone recently showed me footage of us that day, and it looks as crazy as I remember it. Besides the pleasant shock of 80,000 fans going nuts, my next strongest impression was the sharp pain in my ribs: the stage seemed as big as a football field, and we were doing

our normal stage thing of running back and forth like nuts. I was completely winded by the middle of the first song, but had way too much adrenaline to slow down.

Afterwards I found out I had personally garnered another title that day: "2nd Female to Grace the Stage since Doro". I'm sure there have been many more since me, but it was a newsworthy at the time, and I suppose I was the only female musician there that day. That seems weird now, but at the time it was normal.

After our performance we met Kirk from Metallica, and he invited us to stop by his private tent for Martinis later, which was very cool of him. Next thing you know Skid Row are on stage, and Bas is kicking ass! He owned that day; I have never seen someone so "on" and working a crowd like that. The last thing I remember was watching Metallica from the wings, finally evening, outdoors, lights, action, amazing. A perfect day, if only there had been coffee and breakfast!"

Sean Yseult (White Zombie – Bass)

"The Donington experience was a fantastic dream to me, brought forth by nature spirits, it seems. We flew in the night before from Los Angeles. I was very excited about the event because I have always been intrigued about the "Earth energy secrets" for which Donington is well known. Plus, I dig the shit out of castles (who doesn't?). Ideally, I would have liked to share a snifter of brandy next to a lit fireplace with Diane Cilento and Christopher Lee, singing dirty limericks in the

gatehouse, but hey, I'm like Wickerman damaged (I fucking love that movie). As it happened, we flew in and were on early. The time window was so short that we literally had to leave for home almost immediately after the show.

I do remember Slash and I hanging out with Ben Shepherd of Soundgarden sometime before driving to the event. We had a smoke out in the front of the hotel, loitered a bit (like proper rockers should), and then drove to the stage.

I looked out amongst the thousands before our set and thought, "Fuck, yes! This will be a real memory, not some blank weekend warrior recollection!"

We got on with the gig, and I remember that indescribable feeling of energy. It was electrifying and tremendous to play for so many and in such a setting.

We ended our set, said good evening and here comes Metallica!

We then were taken offstage to a V.I.P area somewhere further away (but not behind the stage, so we could still see the show).

I remember a few last things.

I have never heard the real sound of a mechanized armor unit on the move in person before, but from the moment Metallica got on, that's what it sounded like! I dug the hell out of it. It could have caused pensioners and small children to poo themselves! It was that loud right down to the twig and berries chakras. We spent the last while before leaving for the airport chatting in the tent with people, enjoying the English countryside, laughing, a few drinks, kiss kiss. Bye. After the lag wore off in L.A., it was back to 'Eric

Dover, did you pay the electric bill?' and 'Can you run to the bank?' Back to the normal daily affairs. <sigh> For a few weeks afterwards, though, I was still tripping about how whirlwind cool and mythical it was. I would be in a supermarket and look at all the food and think,
"I can BUY ANY of this fucking food I want! I played at Donington, bitches!"
Eric Dover (Slash's Snakepit – Vocals)

"As a kid growing up and listening to rock and metal music, I went to my first Donington in '95; Metallica were headlining with Skid Row, Therapy?, Corrosion Of Conformity and Machine Head and having seen a massive festival like that as a kid, I never thought that I would end up playing it. If someone had come up and told that 13 year old rocker kid that I would have been playing in the same position that Corrosion Of Conformity played, I wouldn't have believed it."
Dave Warsop (Beat Union – Vocals/Guitar)

"I remember this Monsters as it was my first and the one I developed chicken pox at. I got sicker and sicker throughout the day and the noise of the bands did nothing to improve the throbbing pain in my head!!!"
Mike Horton (Plymouth)

"We had not heard about Metallica headlining the 'Escape From The Studio' show in 2005 until late and by then we had made other plans.
To be honest, I do not think that it was organised or announced until fairly late on, which was a shame as it had a pretty damn good line-up."

Roger Moore (Glinton, Peterborough)

"Metallica's fourth appearance saw them headline for the first time and they kicked a bit of life into the old festival with a mixture of old and new numbers (even a couple of brand new songs).
It's a pity I can't say the same about the rest of the day.
As in 1994 bands such as White Zombie and Machine Head were awful to these ears.
Special guest slot was occupied by Therapy?. Not what I would call a Donington band (or not the kind I wanted), but they performed satisfactorily and were OK.
I also enjoyed Slash's Snakepit for their short early in the day slot.
I was the last of the old gang to attend this year. I got a lift with some younger Donington newcomers.
I could sense the old beast was beginning to breathe its last."

Paul Hartshorn (Chesterfield)

"Back in 95 the weather was scorching, (so I remember) anyway, me and a mate had just finished watching Slash's Snake Pit. I was absolutely starving so decided to go grab a bite to eat. We went to the nearest available burger stall. What with Donny's reputation for their 'dethburgers' I ordered 2 hot dogs. Carrying one in each hand. While walking back to where we were sat beforehand walking down a grass verge I felt my legs slip from under me. And landed in the only stretch of mud for miles.

Looked up and there was a single tap water point where the remainder of water had been draining all day and made a mini mud slide. It was about no longer than 7 foot long and a foot wide and I had managed to slip on it. Claire (my mate) laughed hard. To which I received a large cheer and a round of applause from the hundreds of people sat watching me. I took a bow and disappeared rather quickly. My legs / shorts were caked in mud and my mate couldn't stop laughing. In my defence I didn't drop either of my hotdogs though."
Mike Fairhurst (Urmston, Manchester)

1996

Kiss

Ozzy Osbourne, Sepultura, Biohazard, Dog Eat Dog, Paradise Lost, Fear Factory

2nd Stage

Korn

Type O Negative, Everclear,

3 Colours Red, Honeycrack, Cecil

This year saw the return of the second stage and also the return of Kiss as joint headliners with Ozzy Osbourne, who was also making his 3rd visit. The line-up for the day was very diverse, especially across the acts on the mainstage. Opening with the 'industrial metal' of Fear Factory and having Dog Eat Dog's 'nu metal rap crossover' hybrid playing later that afternoon, no one could complain about the lack of variety on offer.

Early afternoon saw the British 'gothic metal' band Paradise Lost draw a considerable crowd and include in their set tracks from their album 'Draconian Times' which had been released 2 months earlier.

After Dog Eat Dog, Biohazard returned to Donington after their truncated set on the second stage in 1995.

The show for Sepultura was a very strange and sad one. Max Cavalera's step son had been killed in an accident and so rather than cancel the show and let down any of their growing legion of fans, Andreas Kisser stepped up to the mark and sang all the songs for the set instead. Max stayed at home, to be near his family.

Over on the second stage there were performances from Cecil (whatever happened to them?), Honeycrack and 3 Colours Red, who have both since split up; the members of Honeycrack have gone on to other careers, Hugo Degenhardt the is now playing the part of Ringo Starr in the Bootleg Beatles, CJ is in the Wildhearts and Willie Dowling is writing music for TV shows and films.

Elsewhere on the 2nd stage, Everclear, the multi million selling 'alt rock' band from Portland, Oregon, USA, put on a fantastic show and were a big success on the day.

Also gaining many fans were Type O Negative, putting in a rare appearance on the day; playing a whole set that only consisted of three songs over a period of 30 minutes, but what a great 30 minutes they were.

Finally the 2nd stage came to a close with Korn, who at the time were a very much 'underground' act and won over the crowd; who couldn't love a band with a dreadlocked bagpipe player?

On the mainstage Ozzy preceded his set with a montage of amusing video clips, with him superimposed in famous historical clips and music videos.

Always a popular choice and making his third appearance at the festival, Ozzy played all the classics 'Iron Man', 'Paranoid' and an encore of 'Crazy Train' and 'Bark At The Moon'; he would return to headline the Ozzfest day at Download 2005, 9 years later.

Finally, Kiss were back, this time with full make up, the original line-up and a set that featured all the classic Kiss songs. Playing a twenty songs set, with music only from their 'make up days', Kiss proved why they were a band at the top of the rockpile and put on one of the most amazing shows ever seen at the festival. Starting with 'Deuce' and ending with 'Rock And Role All Nite', the crowd was entertained by the worlds number one showband; it would be another 12 years before Kiss would return and by then Peter Criss and Ace Frehley would both have been replaced in the band.

So that was it, the final Monsters Of Rock at Donington. Going out on a high, with a double headline slot was a great way to end to an iconic festival, though it would return in a slightly different guise at the Milton Keynes Bowl in 2006.

"I remember being on stage and I thought I was seeing amazing kind of special effect, twirling through the air, but it was water bottles filled with piss."
Paul Stanley (Kiss – Vocals / Guitar)

"Donington was a major part of breaking our career here in Europe.
I remember that at our first show in '96, there was a big lead up to it with 'Korn's coming, Korn's coming', thanks to Rob Flynn from Machine Head who was talking us up a lot in the press, in Kerrang! and a lot of other magazines. He was saying 'you've gotta hear this band called Korn, you've gotta check 'em out', so there was this buzz going round about us.

That was really our 'coming out'. We had come over before with Primus and nobody really knew who we were, but Donington was the show that really blew the doors wide open for us; there was no turning back after that show.
It was a magic show, a funny show that I will never forget."
Jonathan Davis (Korn - Vocals)

"At this time in our career, Dog Eat Dog was used to playing large festivals, but sharing the stage with two of our all time favorite bands, KISS and OZZY, was a dream come true!
It was like a big party with our friends Biohazard, Fear Factory, and Sepultura also on the bill. Add in the beautiful weather and this was a day we'll never forget. I got to shake Gene Simmons and Paul Stanley's hands as they walked thru the backstage. John got to meet Ozzy. Everyone was happy. This was one of the most important shows in DED's history and we will always remember it fondly."
Dave Neabore (Dog Eat Dog - Bass)

"First of all I was so stoked to play with Ozzy and Kiss, being a kid of the 70s and 80s; Kiss were there and I had an all access pass. All I knew about our stage was this band from Cali called Korn was gonna play after us.
The year had been a whirlwind of radio/summer festivals. We had no pull in Europe but things were going well for us in the States.
When asked to do the show I jumped at the chance while the rest of the band resisted. I was a HUGE

*KISS fan and knew that Ace was gonna be on the grounds.
So we set up, got everything in place and I remember seeing people drink alcohol or something out of what looked like plastic pouches. Ok... your gonna be there all day bring your own drink, I thought. Our crew began to set everything up. Korn was to go after us and they were very stoked to play, Munky and I hung out for a while, super cool guy!!!
I think the crowd was ready for Korn but we were next. So while our crew was setting up a few, maybe 3-4 people threw their bags on stage hitting our trusty road crew. They wandered off stage asking, "Why would they throw beer at us?" Well... after they finish drink the beer/alcohol from the bags... it becomes somewhere to piss. Our road crew became targets for their piss bags. Not sure why?
I also hear that Ozzy was not singing that day and there was a guy under the stage singing for him. I was back stage "MAIN STAGE" and saw two young women holding ACE up cuz he was sooooo fuckedup. GENE and PAUL came out and were the usual freaks, Gene looking for girls and Paul looking for guys."*

Craig Montoya (Everclear – Bass)

*"We played the last ever Donington Monsters of Rock Festival, the headliners were Kiss.
It was an amazing event to be part of as the Monsters of Rock Festival was something everyone dreamt of doing in those days.
Our label at the time was Music For Nations. They had a tent set up for us backstage in which*

everything was black; food, drink, everything, pure Spinal Tap and the black sandwiches weren't very popular.
It was also an honour to be playing the main stage. The show was awesome. A sea of people and even some banners just for little, old us."
Gregor Mackintosh (Paradise Lost - Guitar)

"Donington meant everything to me, I remember watching AC/DC and Van Halen being interviewed by Andy Kershaw for the Whistle test in 1984, also, my old man would drive us up from Devon as a kid some years, one of my earliest memories...
So to get the chance to play there was almost other worldly, 3 Colours Red, to my knowledge were either the first, or one of the first bands to play the event as an unsigned act, I think it was '96 so it was a bit nerve wracking, the crowd were well up for it which was great because we were brand new. I remember looking at the massive tyre and being at a loss as to what to say for once, so I tried the line - 'knowing us 3 Colours Red, knowing you Donington', the whole crowd shouted 'A-HAAAAAAAAAAAA'... Awesome."
Pete Vuckovic (3 Colours Red – Vocals/Bass)

"My main memory of Donington is of seeing Kiss' helicopter fly in and land backstage, and later on watching them tottering towards the stage on their platform shoes in full rig, thinking "Wow. That's Kiss". Our time onstage was just a blur of adrenalin. And volume, of course."
Hugo Degenhardt (Honeycrack – Drums/Vocals)

"I couldn't go that year; but I remember when I was a kid taping the rock show on Radio One and Max from Sepultura's step son had just been killed and I remember Andreas doing all the singing for them and it was amazing."
Tom Lacey (The Ghost Of A Thousand – Vocals)

"My first experience of Donington was a near-death one aged 16 at Monsters Of Rock 1996.
My mate Simon and I crawled a quarter mile through a trench that ran under the security fencing and found ourselves in the VIP area - Valhalla to a young metal kid!
After drinking more free booze than we could handle, and making acquaintance with members of Cradle Of Filth and Anathema, we all decided to go back to the main arena to watch Kiss, but got caught in a dust storm as their helicopter landed.
We just lay on the floor until the explosions (they had a LOT of pyro) stopped, and got up shaking, with sand, mud and shit in our hair. Then we watched Kiss jump out of said helicopter.
That event pretty much solidified my entire future, and I've been lost in rock ever since."
Adam Sagir (The Noise Cartel)

"The next trip was 1996 - The Ozzy/Kiss double header. This time it was a minibus full of drunken idiots and a lunatic for a driver. I was married by this time and we all got picked up in the early hours. A crate of beer in the back and a few "herbal" cigarettes going round meant we were in fine spirits when we arrived. The sun was shining, a first for my Donington

trips I believe, and we got to the gate. "Can't bring bottles in" said the guard, offering us a plastic bag with a tap on it "but you can have a couple of these for a quid each."

Decanting our various bottles and cans into these, which looked suspiciously like a bag of piss, we made our way in. To be honest, the drink we'd had on the way down means that it wasn't the most active or memorable of MOR's. My "Donington moment" seemed odd with a second stage at the top of the hill. We found a spot about halfway back, basking in the sun and just drinking in the atmosphere.

Shops made a welcome addition to the burger vans, and I ended up buying my wife a pair of leather trousers. Burger vans were being edged out by Noodle bars - what variety.

Biohazard were ok, Sepultura were impressive if incomplete - Max was absent due to the death of his stepson - and I remember lying down half asleep while Ozzy was on.

Everyone in the group got bored watching Kiss - who were doing a much bigger show than in '88 - and we left before the crush at the end of their set and watched the fireworks from the van. I don't think we even bothered to check out the second stage at all. I mean, who the hell were Korn?

And that was Monsters Of Rock. Time went by, I got divorced. After a fallow period with music, I started listening to new music again.

Phil Hull (Download Forum Administrator)

"Kiss had reunited for their 'Alive' world tour, and were in full makeup; what an iconic performance.

Ozzy's performance, despite the fact that he looked like he could have done with some sort of assistance walking, was also amazing."
Mike Horton (Plymouth)

"August 17th 1996 could not come round quick enough for us, the main reason was a one word reason - KISS. Yes, we had seen KISS four times previously but this was different, this was the original line-up reformed with full makeup and 'Alive' era stage show to boot. This was great news and only got better when it was announced that Ozzy would be co-headlining (although his set was really only a 'special guest' spot). From then on I was not bothered who else got booked, these two were enough for me, in fact when the rest of the bill was announced I could not be bothered with any of them, Fear Factory aside.

In reflection, I think that for us the last few years Monsters Of Rock bills were far inferior to the mega line-ups of '84 and '88, they had more bands with the two stages but we found the under card to be somewhat lightweight. I do not blame the organisers for this, I think that it was as a result of Grunge which had destroyed the Glam scene and was steadily destroying everything else 'Metal' in its wake. To be honest, if the Headliners had not been great, we may have missed '94 and '96, this would have been bad looking back at it now, as we had no idea that they would be the last two under the MOR banner (although I am still unsure whether '96 was called MOR as the ticket just says Donington '96).

We arrived late again that year, about halfway through Dog Eat Dog's set, I was only disappointed that we did not miss their entire set as their Metal/Rap crossover was definitely not my cup of tea. In recent years I have come to appreciate some of the bands who fuse Metal and Rap (Linkin Park, Bodycount and Stuck Mojo to name but three) but in those days I considered it sacrilege, shit! I was still smarting over the whole Aerosmith - Run DMC thing.

After a quick mosey round the stalls and obligatory wait around while the ladies joined the ridiculously long toilet queue, we headed over to the second stage to catch Type-O-Negative.

This year they had moved the second stage around so that it had the back of the stage facing the main stage; I am not sure why they did that? Maybe they found that this afforded better views or less sound leakage in the wind? I have to say, I was impressed with Type-O-Negative, their doomy, gothicky music appealed to me in a kind of Sabbath meets Sisters of Mercy way and their giant vocalist Pete Steel had the right type of deep voice that complemented their sound. I cannot remember what they played apart from 'My Girlfriends Girlfriend' but they hit the spot enough to ensure that I would buy their next three albums.

My opinion of Biohazard had not changed since their last visit in '94, so the chances of me giving them any time was nil. Unfortunately, with no other band playing on another stage at the same time, to drown them out it was impossible to escape from having to hear them. I promised my ears that they would get a treat later for having to suffer this annoying din.

I had heard some rumours about this band Korn and some bloke who plays bagpipes but had not actually heard them. Due to some kind of vote within Kerrang!, Korn were chosen to headline the second stage, this was odd to say the least for an up and coming act, however, on the day there was a huge crowd trying to watch them; we went over but could not see anything, instead we resigned to sitting as close as we could to listen. What I heard was slightly different and definitely something new; in fact I could not decide whether or not I liked it? However, I thought that the fact that I definitely did not hate it was a plus sign, about five years later I brought their back catalogue and liked at least 50% of the material! There was one thing for certain, the huge crowd that were trying to squeeze in front of this relatively small stage were loving it, and the band responded in kind with the most energetic performance I ever saw them play. I think that this performance broke Korn in the UK and from that day on they appear to have almost secured a residency at the venue as not many Download festivals go by without them on the bill or a Korn solo project.

We were only half watching/ listening when Sepultura came on however, this time it was minus frontman Max Cavalera? We were advised that his absence was due to a personal matter that had forced him to return to Brazil, we later discovered that this was due to the tragic death of his stepson in a car accident. I was still not a fan of Sepultura but I admired the fact that despite what must have been an event that affected them all, they soldiered on with Andreas Kisser taking on the vocal duties.

'96 was another Donington day when the weather was good, from what I remember all day. And who better to watch on a hot summer's day than Ozzy! The Oz man has always had a penchant for slinging buckets of water at the crowd, this is usually welcomed by those hot, sweaty individuals at the front but those of us further back usually remain dry. Ozzy being a creative individual had remedied age old problem of soaking us stood further afield on this day by purchasing a water cannon, what a genius, he regularly doused us down and I am sure kept several people from flaking out. I have always been glad that Ozzy has his obsession with this particular element and not any of the other two!

Before Ozzy came on we got a five or so minute video of various famous film scenes with Ozzy appearing in them, including him knocking on the window of Apollo 13 trying to get in, this was a great way to start the set and got everyone in high spirits. Ozzy bounced on to the stage shortly after the vid and treat us to his usual greatest hits style set with a couple of new tracks (I remember 'Perry Mason' I think but none of the others). He was as enthusiastic as ever and kept telling us over and over that he loved us (as usual); his singing was not as good as I have heard on other occasions but this was easy to forgive when the set is good and the band having such a good time. I have seen Ozzy many times as a solo artist and with Sabbath and he has never given anything less than 100%, he is a man possessed on stage with boundless energy and a joy to watch.

During the interval it was time to get on with the usual chores i.e. replenish the beer supply and drain the all ready consumed beverages, I considered this to be absolutely essential on this occasion as I did not want to miss a single minute of today's headliners set. Due to the queues myself and a not to be named acquaintance decided that we could not risk waiting any longer so we decided to use a security fence as a plan B. As we reached the fence there was no sign of any unwanted security so we went about our business watering the said fence and chatting. Before we had finished a whirring noise started and a KISS helicopter appeared (from behind the stage I think) this was of course a signal to get back to our group, I quickly zipped up, but my slower friend was still in mid flow when from out of the darkness leapt a gigantic Rottweiler and hit the fence at with such impact that it knocked my friend over. I picked him up and we headed back into the crowd, however, he was obviously a bit stunned? When I questioned "what the fucks' up with you" he informed me that the friendly canine had missed biting off his old man by centimetres, he swore he felt the mutts nose on his lucky love gun, a lesson had been learned.

We luckily found our group where we had left them just in time for KISS to hit the stage. For most of the next 90 minutes we were treated to the best visual display I had ever seen, this was light years away from their '80's incarnation, just simply stunning.

We got the whole package, Gene breathing fire and spewing fake blood from his platform that he fly's to at the top of the stage, we had Ace firing Rockets from his guitar, we got elevating drum kits, platforms than swing out over the crowd and more pyros than you can shake a stick at. The set list did not

disappoint either, it was all old stuff such as 'Deuce', 'Hotter Than Hell', 'Detroit Rock City', 'Beth', ' I Was Made For Lovin You' and of course finished off with 'Rock n Roll All Nite'. They came, they saw, and on that night (for me anyway) they ruled."
Roger Moore (Glinton, Peterborough)

"My memory of Donington at its best - dodging the dodgy content bottles that always got thrown!
Seriously, I really miss Monsters of Rock! They had the best acts and the best newcomers for you to see first hand.
My best bands have got to be Skin, White Zombie, Metallica and Pride & Glory - they were all fantastic live!"
Gill Talbot (Gravesend, now Carlisle)

"Apart from the co-headliners in 1996, KISS and OZZY, once again there wasn't too much on offer for me during the day. But I rallied myself to go (it was now mainly because I had been to all the previous ones and didn't want to miss it…I was clinging on to my youth….I was now 33 years old).
I travelled down with a new group of festival goers (which included John Slater guitarist-to-be with Blaze Bayley's band after his departure from Iron Maiden. John lived in the same village as me).
The beer flowed quite freely and I must admit I really enjoyed my last Donington.
I went down the front for both Ozzy and KISS and had a great time, the downside being that I lost my camera in the melee at the front shortly after the start of the KISS set.

If Donington was going to go out with a bang rather than a whimper then I suppose KISS in full reunion make-up were the right band to do it. Their stage show is legendary and spectacular 'Rock 'n' Roll All Nite'.

So there you have it, my brief memories of THE MONSTERS OF ROCK festival at Castle Donington 1980 to 1996.

I wonder how many other people attended all fifteen shows…..maybe someone could arrange a reunion…..who knows."

Paul Hartshorn (Chesterfield)

*"I remember the first year Monsters of Rock had two stages, one of my mates scooted off to watch one of the bands on the 2nd stage and came running back to grab us; all he said was "Shit man you won't believe it ya gotta see this band, the lead singer is playing the f#*king bagpipes!?!" Hence to say this was our introduction to Korn!*

I could name so many amazing bands I have seen over the years, I feel so privileged to have been a part of Donington so many times, with so many friends. The atmosphere never fails to make the hairs on the back of my neck stand up, and on those barmy hot days when you're sitting in a field with like minded people, a cold beer in your hand watching and listening to music you love, you will never experience a feeling like it."

Jude Wright (Wallasey, Merseyside)

2006
Monsters of Rock
Deep Purple
Alice Cooper, Journey, Thunder, Queensryche, Ted Nugent, Roadstar

Returning after a 10 year break with a move to a new location, Monsters Of Rock was back. The festival was now based at Milton Keynes Bowl, the site of other massive rock gigs such as Metallica's 'Big Day Out' and the Bon Jovi 'New Jersey' gig.

Blessed with a beautiful sunny day with temperatures in the high 80's, the Gods Of Rock were certainly shining down on the festival; an abundance of red faces were in attendance all day.

First band on were Roadstar (now Heavens Basement), managed by Laurie Mansfield one time guitarist of the band More who had played in 1981 at Donington, they fitted the 'Classic Rock' style perfectly and went

down well with the early afternoon crowd.

Next up, making a rare UK appearance was the 'Motor City Madman', the man who brought us 'Wango Tango', the Nuge himself, Ted Nugent. Trail blazing his way through his extensive back catalogue, Nugent was a big success on the day, with more guitar licks than you could shake a hunting rifle at. The applause was well deserved and Nugent could have played much higher on the bill, perhaps another time at Download?

Queensryche played next and as with their previous appearance at Donington, some of their atmosphere and grandiose stylings were lost in the open air, in the middle of a hot and sunny afternoon. Definitely better in a hot and sweaty club, Queensryche put in a career spanning set with many tracks from the classic 'Operation Mindcrime' album, which has always been a crowd pleaser.

British classic rock on a sunny afternoon in late June, what could be better? And Thunder was the band to fill that gap. Always a good band live and Danny Bowes had a voice that could belt them out with the best. A band that also featured two amazing rock guitarists in Ben Matthews and Luke Morley, a great bass player in Chris Childs and Harry James, a drummer who was splitting his career between Thunder and Magnum, keeping time at the back; what a perfect combination and a winning formula.

This was the 3rd appearance at Monsters Of Rock for Thunder and on the day it was only them and Queensryche that had actually played at Donington before; Thunder would return to Donington for their final
appearance at Download 2009 as part of their final tour.

Next on the line-up was the much anticipated return to the UK for Journey, the 'Kings Of AOR'. Having rarely performed in the UK, in recent years, it was great to see a band as polished as Journey, with Steve Augeri on lead vocals, playing one of his final shows with the band. Journey would search on Youtube and find their next singer Arnel Pineda, in a Journey tribute band in the Philippines; this would be the line-up that would make their Donington debut at Download 2009.

Having never, surprisingly, played at Monsters Of Rock before, Alice Cooper was always going to be a very popular choice for the 'special guest' slot. Featuring all the stage props, from guillotines, to straight jackets, to swords and Alice Cooper Dollar bills, entertainment was the name of the game and Alice was at the top of his. Having played live for nearly 40 years, his show was perfectly executed, as was Alice with the
guillotine. His daughter also took part in the stage show and was stabbed through with a

sword, a befitting way for Alice to treat his offspring.
After the theatrical performance of Mr Cooper anything that followed had a lot to live up to, but with classic tunes and a superstar band, Deep Purple filled the headline slot with plenty of energy, passion and great entertainment.
The crowd did 'thin out' a bit after Alice Cooper's set, but that was understandable due to the young crowd in attendance, but what could beat classics like 'Black Knight' and of course 'Smoke On The Water' playing in a field on a balmy summers evening.
Monsters Of Rock was back and with a vengeance, less of a capacity than in previous years at Donington, but popular all the same. MOR would come back amalgamated into the Download bill on the Sunday.

"Monsters of Rock at Milton Keynes, the atmosphere was exciting, I felt this 'buzz' all day long and it was one of the best vibes; EVER."
Ian Gillan (Deep Purple - Vocals)

"The good thing about playing these festivals is you're always getting to play with old friends. When you've been round for thirty five to forty years, everybody on the bill is someone you know or someone you've played with before. Whether it's Deep Purple or some of the older bands it's fun for us.
We never change our show ever; it's always going to

be the same show. So we get up and look at the bill and say 'Who's on tonight'. I remember one night we played with Arthur Brown who I hadn't seen since 1968 and he came back and he looked better than he did in '68!! It's great to see bands like that, bands that we learned from and that is the coolest thing, playing with old friends.
We do have total respect for any band that we play with, but it's kinda unfair for the band that comes on after us, because of all the production. We went out on a twin bill with Deep Purple, in Europe and I wasn't sure how they were going to fare after the guillotines and the confetti, but I have to say that they are better now than they were then."
Alice Cooper (Alice Cooper - Vocals)

"It was a message from God himself, he turned the lights on and this was the first nice day of the year really.
I thought about a week before, no it's not going to happen, but it's terrific and I think you need good weather for a festival and I think that it went well."
Luke Morley (Thunder - Guitar)

"We played at Milton Keynes Bowl with Deep Purple and the weather on that day was spectacular and it just makes everybody happy.
There were quite a few lobsters on the way home, people getting caught in the field and going bright red."
Ben Matthews (Thunder - Guitar)

"The weather was good; I don't remember anything that stood out about the day, but I guess nothing went horribly wrong, it's hard to remember details.
It's not the best situation, like your own show. In the States we don't have festivals like that, or the longevity, going on for years and years."
Geoff Tate (Queensrÿche – Vocals)

"The energy and piss and vinegar factors were off the charts, and I heard joyful tales of appreciation for our 1976 Reading rockout every year I return, including when we rocked their brains out again in 2006. The human and musical bond is timeless."
Ted Nugent (Ted Nugent – Guitar / Vocals)

"Well, an interesting thing about our show at M.O.R was that it was only the 2nd show for Syd (our new guitarist). He made his debut the night before at the Pitz when we opened for Diamond Head in a warm up show for the festival. Now the rest of the guys (myself, Jonny, Rob and Richie) had some big stage experience from our supports to Meat Loaf, The Darkness, and Nickelback etc...But Syd had none!
The warm up gig playing to around 300 people was actually the biggest gig he had ever done, until the day after of course when we opened the festival to around 10,000 ha-ha!
We were very happy with our performance, we had a few onstage problems but I guess that's to be expected at a festival! The crowd was great before

we went on and the response as we left the stage, we couldn't have asked for better!

The day in a whole was something we will never forget, we have joined an elite club of bands that have played 'Monsters of Rock' unfortunately we couldn't stick around for 'Purples' set as we had to head up to Manchester to open for Queensryche the following night.. As for Crazyness, hangin' around with the likes of Ted Nugent, Alice Cooper etc was pretty crazy ha-ha!

Chris Rivers (Roadstar – Drums)

"This was our first Monsters Of Rock event and what a line up?

Travelled from Plymouth to Milton Keynes, straight to the hotel then taxi to the venue. Arrived at the Bowl and the music had already started by Roadstar.

After checking out the merchandise and sinking a few beers it was on with the music. Waiting to see the great man himself Ted Nugent and he did not let us or the crowd down, with classics like 'Cat Scratch Fever' and 'Wango Tango'.

Followed by Queensrÿche, then Thunder......what great sounds from groups that we never had in our record collection. A top up of more beer then some noodles and we were then ready for Journey.

Journey played all the classic tracks like 'Don't Stop Believin', 'Any Way You Want It' and 'Separate Ways' with singer Steve Augeri. Not the same vocal range as Steve Perry, but a great show.

Alice Cooper followed, with all the great on stage show antics. He still rocks!

After some late supper, it was on to Deep Purple. This was the second time of seeing Deep Purple and they still rocked, with classic songs like 'Smoke On The Water' and songs from 'Rapture Of The Deep' album. The crowd had reached about 20,000 and the bowl was shaking.

Deep Purple was a great finale to a great event and venue. We were hoping for a follow up seeing this was the first Monsters of Rock for 10 years but this never followed at Milton Keynes Bowl."

Mark & Jane Jewitt (Plymouth)

Printed in Great Britain
by Amazon.co.uk, Ltd.,
Marston Gate.